MARVELS AND MIRACLES IN
LATE COLONIAL MEXICO

A Volume in the

RELIGIONS OF THE AMERICAS SERIES

Sacred Spaces and Religious Traditions in Oriente Cuba
by Jualynne E. Dodson

Louis Riel and the Creation of Modern Canada:
Mythic Discourse and the Postcolonial State
by Jennifer Reid

Strange Jeremiahs: Civil Religion and the Literary Imaginations
of Jonathan Edwards, Herman Melville, and W. E. B. Du Bois
by Carole Lynn Stewart

Shrines and Miraculous Images:
Religious Life in Mexico Before the Reforma
by William B. Taylor

Editors: DAVÍD CARRASCO AND CHARLES H. LONG

Marvels & Miracles in
Late Colonial Mexico

THREE TEXTS IN CONTEXT

William B. Taylor

UNIVERSITY OF NEW MEXICO PRESS
Albuquerque

© 2011 by the University of New Mexico Press
All rights reserved. Published 2011
Printed in the United States of America
16 15 14 13 12 11   1 2   3 4 5 6

Library of Congress Cataloging-in-Publication Data
Taylor, William B.
Marvels and miracles in late colonial Mexico:
three texts in context / William B. Taylor.

p. cm. — (Religions of the Americas)
Includes bibliographical references and index.
ISBN 978-0-8263-4975-0 (cloth : alk. paper)
1. Miracles—Mexico—Early works to 1800.
2. Mexico—Church history—18th century—Sources.
I. Title.
II. Title: Trouble with miracles.
III. Title: Our lady in the kernel of corn.
IV. Title: Between Nativitas and Mexico City.
BT97.3.T39 2011
232.91'70972—dc22

2010040720

$\mathcal{C}$ONTENTS

FOREWORD

With the publication of *Marvels and Miracles in Late Colonial Mexico: Three Texts in Context*, our Religions of the Americas series offers an innovation to benefit readers who want to go more deeply into the history of religion in Mexico. This sourcebook is a companion volume to William B. Taylor's *Shrines and Miraculous Images: Religious Life in Mexico Before the Reforma* and consists of three substantial, largely ignored documents about miracles and shrines in late colonial Mexico, plus introductory essays on faith practices and colonial politics. It provides for students of colonial Mexico important primary sources and invites them to enter more vigorously into dialogues about historical understandings of religious devotion and practice in Mexico. The three documents, in Taylor's words, help us "glimpse news of miracles in their first, unfinished stages—more singular and idiosyncratic in ways that restore some rough edges, personalities, and contingencies to the compressed, authorized miracle stories." Taylor views historical writing as, in part, "a restless kind of discipline of context," and readers of this book will benefit from his disciplined work on the sensual faith of Catholic Christianity and the ways this sensual faith was transmitted, received, and reworked by people in various social and political positions. Through Taylor's dexterous ways of handling these documents, we are able to move closer to what was considered crucial to the personal and collective well-being of Mexico and Mexicans. We hope that this innovation of combining primary documents with interpretive essays in a single volume will lead to other skillful advances in scholarship on the many religious practices and traditions in this part of the Americas.

—Davíd Carrasco
Harvard University

Acknowledgments

*S*pecial thanks to my students and coteachers in History 8A and 140A at the University of California, Berkeley, who worked through these and other primary sources with me.

I am indebted to the Fondo Reservado of the Biblioteca Nacional de México on the campus of the Universidad Nacional Autónoma de México for permission to publish my translation of "History of Miracles Worked by the Image of Our Lady of Intercession which is Venerated in the Monastery of Nativitas" and the accompanying print; to the Bancroft Library for permission to include my translation of "Summary investigation concerning the marvel that Our Lady of the Walnut Tree"; to *The Americas: A Quarterly Review of Inter-American Cultural History* for permission to republish "Our Lady in the Kernel of Corn" from vol. 59:4 (April 2003), pp. 559–70; to the University of New Mexico Press for "Between Nativitas and Mexico City: Miracles and the Mundane in an Eighteenth-Century Pastor's Local Religion," which first appeared in Martin Nesvig, ed., *Local Religion in Colonial Mexico* (Albuquerque: University of New Mexico Press, 2006), pp. 91–117; and to Koninklijke Brill N.V. for permission to include "Trouble with Miracles: An Episode in the Culture and Politics of Wonder in Colonial Mexico," from Christopher Ocker, Michael Printy, Peter Starenko, and Peter G. Wallace, eds., *Politics and Reformations: Communities, Polities, Nations, and Empires. Essays in Honor of Thomas A. Brady, Jr.* (Leiden: Brill, 2007), vol. 1, pp. 441–58.

Introduction

*T*he readings in this little book consist of three unusual documents about miracles in late colonial Mexico paired with an introductory essay. The documents date from the second half of the eighteenth century when Spain's Bourbon dynasty sought to tighten its control over the New World colonies in ways meant to reform imperial institutions and change the role of the church and religion in colonial life. As the essays suggest, these documents bear on colonial politics and society, as well as faith in practice; and each one is rich and ambiguous enough to include distinctive voices and open complex episodes that invite more than one line of inquiry without final answers.

Miracles—those signs of divine presence and intervention in the world that defy ordinary experience of cause and effect[1]—have been esteemed by Christians, especially Catholic Christians, as a central belief and treated as allegories of salvation. Christian shrines are almost always miracle shrines, and miracles became one more proof that "our religion is a living one," as Mexican Jesuit Francisco de Florencia put it near the end of the seventeenth century. While God was believed to have unlimited power to work wonders in the world, miracles were recognized and publicized sparingly by the church hierarchy during Mexico's colonial period. "Miracle" was a loaded word, with juridical meaning—only a bishop's court could say whether a portentous occurrence truly was a miracle. The colonial courts usually were silent on the matter, then increasingly reluctant to recognize miracles during the late eighteenth century when the three documents in this book were composed.

After the Council of Trent (1545–1563), Catholic leaders were inclined to regard Christ's displays of wonder working in the New Testament as the necessary cornerstones of Christianity's beginning rather than the first of countless miracles to come. Their view was that miracles were still possible, but less common, both because the true Church was established

1

and because the faith of most Christians had cooled and no longer invited personal intervention. Or, if supernatural events did occur, they were likely to be the work of the devil, leading the morally weak astray and endangering their immortal souls. By the eighteenth century, more direct documentation of miraculous events was expected and many colonial officials took a more skeptical stance, often dismissing the growing number of reported wonders as overripe fruit of popular ignorance and superstition or mendacity. With or without official encouragement, news of amazing healings, rescues, and acts of divine retribution broke and surged like ocean waves on a rising or ebbing tide throughout Mexico's long colonial period among all kinds of people, but believers learned that it was best to speak of *maravillas* or *prodigios*, and leave the finer points about divine intervention to the courts.

People may not have expected instant miracles in their lives, but many were led to hope, and to practice rituals of appeal and thanks that have left some traces. A long tradition of offering *milagritos*—miniature wax or metal figures, mostly of body parts, that served as tokens of prayer for supernatural favor—provides many examples and early references, but the cloud of undated anonymity surrounding them rarely can be penetrated. The written record of experiences of wonder in early Mexico is equally elusive, even when judicial inquiries about them (*informaciones jurídicas*) were undertaken in the seventeenth and eighteenth centuries. Often the truth claims for miracles rested more on popular acclaim—the *voz pública y fama*—than on concrete evidence from the time and place. As the first essay ("Trouble with Miracles") explains, most of the reports of divine intervention that have come down to us are abbreviated, conventional descriptions, a few lines in length, published in novena booklets and devotional histories with the approval of the bishop's court, or a precious few ex-voto paintings with short captions that were originally displayed on church walls near a favorite religious image. In various ways, all were filtered through lenses of ecclesiastical authority. They are products of substantial editing and simplification, a process Aron Gurevich discovered for medieval Europe in the visions of two peasant men at the turn of the thirteenth century. In his vision, Gottschalk of Holstein "saw a tree on whose branches grew boots for the souls of the departed, since they must cross a field strewn with terrible thorns. Then he came to a stream in which sharp weapons were floating, and only those souls who climbed on to rafts could escape mutilation. Finally, he came to a crossroads with three paths to which an angel was directing souls." Gottschalk added details about relations with his neighbors and other mundane concerns, "for which he was reproached by the priest who wrote down his narrative." Thurkill of Essex spoke of his vision in 1206 only "in fragments, recalling this or that episode and omitting and passing over much in silence. Then, after talking with the parish priest, who probably gave him the necessary directions, Thurkill's story acquired coherence and fullness. It was this finished, 'redacted' form that Thurkill repeated to his fellow parishioners and lord, and in the monasteries to which he was invited; it was this version that was written down." In both cases, the story acquired focus and a clear, concise narrative line with the help of a priest. As Gurevich says, "In this way, the vision passed through a sort of ecclesiastical censorship and was brought into accord with received tradition. [T]he vision as a fact of popular culture could not be fixed; it had to be included within ecclesiastical tradition. Only in a certain symbiosis with learned tradition could medieval popular tradition exist."[2]

If the hundreds of authorized thumbnail stories of amazing events associated with ardent appeals to Christ and the saints or a spiritual exercise such as the rosary are considered together, some tantalizing patterns surface. A family resemblance to European miracle stories is not surprising since miracles are about a universal longing for wholeness and health in literal and allegorical ways, and Iberian sources were the familiar models. Like their European counterparts, most of the Mexican miracles involved relief from life-threatening or crippling conditions—acute illness, blindness, deafness, paralysis, serious accidents, flood, fire, lightning, earthquake, and famine. Many of these restorative miracles replay the New Testament miracle stories of Christ's resurrection, healing touch, and promise of salvation—restoring sight and hearing, casting out demons, and calming storms. As in Europe, some Mexican miracle shrines and divine personages specialized in particular kinds of favors or reflected their time and place in definite ways—protecting travelers and fishermen on the water or workers in the mines; calming an unruly horse or a raging bull in a ranching region; warding off a rabid dog in town or robbers on the thoroughfares of trade and travel. The specialty of other incarnations of divine presence had a more universal ring—Our Lady of Sorrows aiding women in the throes of childbirth; Our Lady of the Remedies bringing life-giving rain; St. Joseph mitigating destructive lightning strikes; various saints and advocations of Mary and Christ curing the blind and protecting against epidemic disease; and Our Lady of Zapopan ensuring a good death by forewarning devotees that their time of reckoning was near. But in contrast to the usual European patterns, miracle stories for colonial Mexico focused on images that showed signs of life and wielded power over nature. Few captivity tales appear among the Mexican miracles, and they are less fraught with political and social danger. Nearly all the Mexican miracles favored righteous believers, whereas more of the European miracles, especially from earlier centuries, favored the less worthy in ways that emphasized God's grace over good works of the devout. Somewhat more men than women were the beneficiaries of these colonial Mexican miracles, but there was a relatively equal distribution in contrast to the male-dominated medieval European miracles or the nineteenth-century French miracle sets where women were overwhelmingly favored. When the Mexican miracles identified beneficiaries by social rank elites were overrepresented, but all classes of people were included.

The founding miracles of Iberian and Mexican shrines also were quite similar. They were place-centered, drawing attention to the specific site of divine presence with celestial music, strange lights, mules or horses bearing religious images that would not budge from the spot or went directly to it, and the chosen images kept returning to the place where they first appeared. Amazingly beautiful images were delivered by angelic young men in white who vanished without a trace, as they did in European origin stories.

Among the shrines dedicated to celebrated images, there are examples of nearly all the types of founding stories of divine presence found in early modern Europe, but with a striking difference. Of the three basic types described by Philip Soergel for European image shrines[3]—holiness tried and triumphant; holiness lost and found; and holiness suddenly revealed in apparitions, activations, and other miracles—the third prevailed in Mexico. In the first type, an image or sacred material resisted desecration and destruction. Infidels or apostates tried to destroy an image or the consecrated Host and were unable to do so. This was a characteristic founding miracle in Soergel's regional study of Bavaria, where the examples centered on the integrity of the Host—Jews and other deniers of Christ tried and failed to destroy the consecrated wafer, although sometimes they made it bleed. The examples of holiness tried and triumphant are rare for New Spain.[4] The second type fits a familiar Spanish pattern described by William Christian: images of Mary hidden by Christians in the countryside during the Muslim conquest of Iberia were discovered thanks to supernatural signs of intense light and celestial music, or a semidomesticated animal like a bull or mule was drawn to the place where the image was then discovered by a shepherd.[5] Again, there are examples of images lost and found among the miracles of origin for New Spain, but they were less common and rarely hidden or abandoned by Christians on the defensive. And many more of the found objects in New Spain were figures of Christ. The third type, of holiness suddenly revealed, is overwhelmingly the most common in

New Spain. In these founding stories, images already in place or arriving in mysterious circumstances showed signs of life or spontaneously began to work miracles. The founding stories of divine presence associated with images both in Spain and New Spain are about place as much as about the image, but the cases in New Spain are less often about conquest, warrior Virgins, and threats to the faith.

Something can be learned from these abbreviated miracle stories as they are, but no matter how numerous, there is no denying that they are not a random or transparently representative group of the miracle episodes that circulated. They are exemplary stories, preselected for us, not case histories; they were shaped in ways that are rarely clear in the written record.[6] And they beg most of the questions about reception and context historians would want to ask: Where have these stories been? That is, who had a hand in their making? How did they take shape? How and by whom were these stories recalled and used? Was there just one, fixed story at the beginning or later? Were other versions remembered and accepted? What about all the silences in them that a generic five-line version glides over? Walt Whitman declared that "it makes such a difference *where* you read."[7] Is location—in place and time—an important aspect of their making, recollection, and meaning? Among all the possible historical contexts in which news of particular miracles circulated, which ones were salient when?

So, the silences in these miracle stories stand out more than the information in them. The process of feedback and alteration glimpsed by Gurevich is missing. Rarely, too, do the recorded stories open out to the contingencies, the social, political, and cultural contexts, and the operation of ecclesiastical courts that would take us deeper into Marian devotion, administrative reforms, gender, class, ethnicity, and faith in practice during the colonial period. These three manuscript records take us partway there, to glimpse news of miracles in their first, unfinished stages—more singular and idiosyncratic in ways that restore some rough edges, personalities, and contingencies to the compressed, authorized miracle stories. They have their silences, too, but they are longer and document more open-ended episodes of conflict and collaboration that reach to and beyond matters of faith and ritual toward the larger social and political history of colonial experience and actors infrequently heard from in the written record. In small, precise ways they also intersect with larger themes of the time and better-known devotions such as burgeoning devotion to Our Lady of Guadalupe, the politics of religion, and assaults on the prominent place of the Franciscans in public life.

PART I

Trouble with Miracles

An Episode in the Culture and Politics of Wonder in Colonial Mexico[1]

*M*iracles have been a defining belief in the history of Christianity. Christian shrines of the Middle Ages and Catholic shrines since the sixteenth century are famous for marvelous healings and protection that mark them as special places of transparency between devotees and the divine. Such supernatural boons to believers "assure the infallibility of our Holy Catholic Faith," wrote the Spanish savant, Benito Jerónimo Feijóo, in the early eighteenth century.[2] "Books" of miracles consisting of hundreds, sometimes thousands, of short entries written down by attending priests as early as the fifth century became a common feature of European shrines in the twelfth and thirteenth centuries, with entries occasionally added through the seventeenth and eighteenth centuries.[3] During the confessional and political upheavals of the Reformation, news of miracles and the record of them mushroomed, leading historian Craig Harline to call seventeenth-century Europe one of the "brightest . . . golden ages and places of miracles."[4] Philip Soergel found a veritable floodtide of miracle events reported at particular German shrines—about 12,000 from Neuhirchen beig Heilig Blut in the seventeenth and eighteenth centuries, and about 16,500 at Bettbrunn from 1573 to 1768.[5] But there was a countervailing development in Catholic Europe during the early modern period that could quiet the exuberant recording and publicizing of miracle stories. The twenty-fifth session of the Council of Trent on December 3–4, 1563, called for "no new miracles [to] be accepted or new relics recognized without the bishop's examination and approval."[6]

Where reformed bishops faced the rise of Protestantism on their doorsteps, they might well risk trying to reinvigorate the faith by encouraging news of new miracles, but in Spain and the Spanish empire the Trent reforms to strengthen the authority and power of the bishops seem to have affected the promotion and dissemination of miracle stories in three ways: (1) the shrine books of miracles often fell out of favor and new entries dwindled or ceased; (2) lengthy inquiries about miracles were undertaken at the bishop's court only in a few special cases, mainly for shrines a bishop meant to promote or to investigate and silence reports of miracles that seemed threatening to the institutional church[7]; and (3) the publication of devotional shrine histories and novena booklets from the late sixteenth century on reduced the number of recognized miracles to a dozen or so exemplary cases.[8] In Mexico, the authors of published devotional texts during the seventeenth and eighteenth centuries who mentioned apparent miracles were careful to speak of *maravillas* (marvels and wonders) and leave the question of whether they were truly miracles to higher authorities.

Miracles were both necessary and troublesome for authorities of the early modern Catholic Church as they worked to contain and direct what Émile Durkheim called the "contagiousness" of the sacred.[9] Miracles validated Christianity as a living faith of transcendent power and protection, but they also spilled out in directions that invited false prophets and undermined the dream of a universal Christian church in a time of sectarian divisions. Max Weber thought that trouble of this kind not only had deep roots in the Christian tradition, but was a perennial challenge to the priesthood of any established religion in its claim to special knowledge and institutional control over access to the divine.[10] As a religion of the book, this tension in Christianity between charismatic powers of would-be prophets and seers and the institutionalized spiritual authority of the priesthood found official expression in the proposition that God has rarely spoken through supernatural phenomena since the time of Christ. If a supernatural event was reported, was it really God's doing or just wishful thinking about an unusual natural event or an illusion concocted by a cunning magician? And if it was judged to be a supernatural event, was it the work of God or Satan? Given these chronic tensions, church authorities were bound to intervene and restrict where they could.

There is trouble, too, for historians of New Spain (early modern Mexico and Central America) who seek to understand what miracles meant to people of the time and how they influenced local practices of faith. Mexico has been described as "a society that devoured news of miraculous events," but the written records about them are thin, scattered, and almost always combed and shaped into a few lines each by ecclesiastical authorities. I have found no "books of miracles" kept at Mexican shrines, no long-running registers of the European kind.[11] The authors of the early devotional histories and novena booklets that set out what became the small canon of miracle stories for a shrine lamented that nearly all the great marvels of the place had gone unrecorded. Except in the shifting sands of pious hearsay, they were lost to posterity.[12]

From the seventeenth century on, historians have been moved by a desire to counter "this epidemic of forgetfulness."[13] The trouble with miracles for historians stems from the trouble with miracles for the authorities and the purging and editing of the written record that followed. Prelates and their priests had good reasons not to publicize the full array of marvels-cum-miracles that circulated by word of mouth and were expressed tangibly, if ephemerally and often inaudibly, in gestures, prayers, and votive offerings at home and in shrines. Both theologically and politically, authorities knew that there could not be many miracles and that true ones conformed to familiar patterns, inspired by the miracles Christ worked in the gospels.

My meager success in trying to establish how miracles were understood and how they influenced the practice of faith in seventeenth- and eighteenth-century Mexico is not because miracles and their reception are rarely mentioned. There are hundreds of references, but as Kenneth Woodward noted for Christian miracle stories in general, they are exemplary stories, not simply case histories. They offer known types, not necessarily representative types.[14] I can do something that feels substantial with the uses of an eighteenth-century devotional print or two (see the essay and document in this volume on Francisco Antonio de la Rosa Figueroa and Our Lady of Intercession) and the patterns of "founding miracle" stories for several dozen Mexican shrines, which are less about the faith and society endangered than most European shrine stories, and more about holiness suddenly revealed in an apparition or a statue that changed posture, grew, or wept. But beyond a few extended investigations of reported miracles by episcopal courts in which the investigators' voices and enthusiasms overwhelm those of devotees, I am stalled by the record of miracle stories for what they meant to those who told and heard of them, and how they circulated and changed. It is not that nothing can be done with the eight hundred or so miracle stories from the colonial period I have collected so far, but eight hundred truncated and scattered stories is not many, and they rarely come in large bunches that are well-contextualized in time and place. Forced onto tables, this selection displays a range of dangers, favors, and preoccupations much like those of their European counterparts, although more men than women are represented in these Mexican stories (by a ratio of about 3:2). Most were cures (252) or narrow escapes from life-threatening situations (217). Nearly half of the cures were for acute internal distress—intestinal complaints in most cases, it appears—followed by recoveries from paralysis (34) and dangerous birthings (34), perhaps also reflecting the most familiar or at least notable maladies of the day.[15] Cases of resuscitation (27), restoration of sight (20), exorcism (15), and recovery from deafness (7) stand out, too, serving as allegories of enlightenment, revelation, and salvation, or reenacting the particular miracles Christ performed in the gospel stories.[16]

People may not have expected instant miracles in their lives, but many were led to hope and to practice rituals of promise, propitiation, and thanks. However, the traces of them are ephemeral and anonymous. Candles, flowers, coins, and little wax or silver body parts called *milagritos* were the common votive offerings of most people.[17] Colonial milagritos are rarely seen today, but they did not usually disappear in some mysterious or irreverent way. Many were recycled—melted down to make candles if they were made of wax, and candlesticks or other religious ornaments if made of silver. More personalized miracle stories favoring the less privileged during the colonial period occasionally turn up in unexpected places, but I have found them mainly in a few lines in devotional histories and novena booklets. Most are generic cures or narrow escapes, but a few are more specific in a homely way: "María de Viscarra of the city of Guanajuato in the neighborhood of San Juan was eating round cactus apples at home and swallowed a spine, which stuck in her throat. She motioned for a print of Our Lady of El Pueblito, which she kept on a small altar, kissed it reverently and coughed up the spine."[18]

Ex-voto paintings are especially approachable, personal artifacts of faith in the miraculous for colonial Mexico. Usually these small paintings on canvas or wooden tablets vividly depict an accident or a sickbed scene. Votive paintings of miracle scenes are not unique to Mexico, of course. The form was introduced from Europe, but had a later and long life in Mexico, enjoying great popularity in the nineteenth century and lasting well into the twentieth. It is part of a tradition that apparently flowered in Italy in the sixteenth century and spread through much of Catholic Europe before declining there in the late nineteenth century. In Mexico during the seventeenth and eighteenth centuries it was an expression of thanks mainly for elites, who could afford to commission them. What appear to be spontaneous expressions of personal devotion and vivid depictions of miraculous cures and rescues are actually quite stylized in their presentations, expressing in a standardized way what people wanted to be seen and recorded. But which people? Who made the choices? Who did the paintings? We can rarely know, beyond the likelihood that few devotees painted their own ex-votos. The challenge of inferring much about popular and personal understandings of miracles from these colonial ex-voto paintings commissioned by elites is compounded by their small number. Fewer than one hundred examples in shrines and private collections have been published—too few to constitute a sample. How many more were destroyed, lost, or have not been published remains an open question. Certainly many fewer were made before the nineteenth century when ex-voto scenes painted on tin became a cottage industry, but even then it is doubtful that the hundreds of nineteenth- and twentieth-century survivors from a particular shrine constitute a representative sample since local pastors would have culled offbeat, crude, decrepit, and otherwise unedifying specimens, and some of the more pleasing pictures found their way into national and international art and artisan markets beginning in the 1920s.[19]

Typically an early ex-voto painting is divided into three registers: the heavenly realm of the devotional image at the top; the miracle scene occupying most of the frame; and a caption at the bottom. Most captions are much like the brief miracle accounts in devotional histories and novena booklets, identifying the grateful devotee, the event, the place, the date, and the object of devotion. An undated but otherwise typical caption reads, "A distinguished Spanish woman, Doña Gerónima de la Llana of Pátzcuaro was acutely ill with a malignant fever. She pleaded for the statue of Our Lady of La Salud (Our Lady of Health) to be brought to her bedside. She prayed fervently to the Virgin Mary and suddenly felt relief. In thanks she offered Our Lady an exquisite new dress and cloak."[20] Like nearly all the others, this record is particular to a place and person, but the pictorial and written representation is standardized and reduced to the essentials.[21]

We say that a picture is worth a thousand words, but I wish we had those thousand words and more from the patrons and painters to go with these paintings. Many of the ex-voto paintings are now in private collections, treated as freestanding art objects, far from their original shrine context. As attractive and individualized as they may be, the paintings are usually no less standardized than the short captions that accompany them. In fact, most of the paintings were meant to illustrate the captions, the artist probably taking his cues in conversation with the devotee who commissioned the painting. Though they have a particular setting, the stories in them are reduced to essentials, expressing familiar types of events, with little about the loose ends and possible ambiguities of the episode. This, in itself, can be revealing—documenting what people wanted to be seen and recorded, especially about the gestures and other conventions of communication with the divine. But, again, which people? Who made the choices? Who chose to preserve the paintings? What is left out? What experiences are hidden under the placid surface of these two- or three-line stories? That is, what is their provenance and how were they viewed? We rarely know.

María Francisca Larralde and Our Lady of the Walnut Tree

"History is made up of episodes," E. P. Thompson suggested, "and if we cannot get inside these, we cannot get inside history at all. This has always been inconvenient to the schematists."[22] Here is a daunting proposition for the history of miracles. Can the surface of an episode like the colonial ex-voto sickbed scene of Doña Gerónima de la Llana and her offering of precious garments be scratched for more than its abbreviated story and fairy-tale ending told by someone else? Hardly ever, it appears, but I recently read an eighteenth-century record that brings me a little closer to a similar episode that was not memorialized in an official publication. This one was right under my nose in an as-yet-uncatalogued box of miscellaneous Mexican manuscripts in UC-Berkeley's Bancroft Library. Here is my reading of the Bancroft document and what it suggests about doubts and certainties of faith in an episode much like many depicted in eighteenth-century ex-voto paintings.[23]

On March 29, 1758, Doña María Francisca Larralde and her husband, Sergeant Major Don Antonio Urresti, citizens of the small city of Monterrey in the far northern province of Nuevo León, sent a file of documents to the bishop of Guadalajara, some three hundred miles away. As they explained in their cover letter, the file contained depositions by dignitaries of their city who witnessed the course of Doña María Francisca's suffering and recovery from a grave illness between December 16, 1757, and February 17, 1758, and the vows she made to Nuestra Señora del Nogal (Our Lady of the Walnut Tree) in the hope of regaining her health and achieving a good death. Now she sought the bishop's judgment on whether she was obliged to fulfill her vows.

The file includes depositions by seven male dignitaries, all of them priests, six of whom were deposed twice. An eighth summary testimony was made in the name of the captain general of the province and other leading citizens. Less than thirty years old (her mother was married in 1728), Doña María Francisca clearly commanded the attention of Monterrey's political and spiritual elite. The priests included the pastor of the city, Licenciado Bartolomé Molano; his two assistant pastors, Joseph Lorenzo Báez de Treviño and Luis Buenaventura de la Garza; her brother, Bachiller Francisco Antonio Larralde, who was the ecclesiastical judge of the district; the retired president and prior of the Franciscan convent, Fray Miguel de la Portilla; another former Franciscan prior, Fray Blas de Quintanilla; and Lic. Don Juan Báez Treviño, the regional commissary of the Inquisition. A silent presence in the documents is Doña María Francisca's mother, Doña Josepha Francisca Cantú del Río y la Zerda, widow of the former military leader of the province, General Don Francisco Ygnacio Larralde, and *mayordoma de la fábrica de la parroquia*—in charge of overseeing funds for improvements to the parish church and promoting the cult of its celebrated image of Our Lady of the Walnut Tree. Doña Josepha Francisca was from a prominent family of Valle de las Salinas, and both she and her sister, María Juliana, had married Basque immigrants who rose to regional prominence.[24] Doña María Francisca was being cared for in her mother's home when the events of late 1757 and early 1758 transpired, and in the second phase of her daughter's recovery Doña Josepha Francisca steered the activity into the city's parish church and Franciscan convent.

The individual depositions can be studied in the translation of the case record that follows. Together they provide a detailed, largely complementary chronicle of events and sentiments, including Doña María Francisca's surprising recovery. To summarize the points of agreement in the depositions, Doña María Francisca became gravely ill in the middle of December 1757, hardly able to eat or drink, and passing in and out of consciousness. Expecting her to die at any moment, one or another of the church dignitaries kept vigil around the clock until January 13. On January 1 the parish priest attended the seemingly lifeless body and called upon Doña María Francisca to squeeze his hand, and she responded. He summoned her mother and brother to witness this happy turn of events. María Francisca recovered full consciousness briefly, making various charitable wishes known, and giving a sign for her husband to come forward. She asked him to grant her permission to take the veil should she recover, to which he agreed. Then she took leave of her household and asked for communion, anticipating her death. She soon fell back into a nearly lifeless state until January 13, 1758, when her mother asked that the sovereign image of Our Lady of the Walnut Tree be brought to her bedside, attended by the priests of the city reciting the litany of the Virgin. Doña Josepha Francisca decorated a portable altar beside her daughter's bed and placed a beautiful string of pearls around the statue's neck that María Francisca had promised to the Virgin. Soon the sick woman lifted her head, and with new strength spoke in praise of the Holy Sacrament, Our Lady of Sorrows, and the sweet names of Jesus, Mary, and Joseph.

I can imagine an ex-voto painting of the event with Doña María Francisca in bed, the statue of Our Lady of El Nogal adorned with the string of pearls, the dignitaries and family members gathered around, and a caption mentioning her illness and giving thanks for her marvelous recovery in the presence of this image of Mary. But there is more to the episode. Doña María Francisca asked that the church bells of the city be rung to honor God and remind the citizens that their continuing misfortunes stemmed from tepid devotion to the Divine Lady, and declaring that her own misfortune resulted from having turned away from her early desire to lead a celibate life as a bride of Christ. She took her husband's hand and asked him to affirm her recent vow of celibacy, asked him to dress in the habit of a Franciscan for two years, and to allow her to make a pilgrimage to Our Lady of Guadalupe at her shrine near Mexico City, walking the last three leagues. To all this, he once again agreed.

On February 7, however, she again became deathly ill, immobile and unable to take even a sip of water. On February 17 her mother, brother, and husband decided to take her to the altar of Our Lady of the Walnut Tree in the parish church. At about ten in the morning, the priests of the city carried her there on a stretcher, chanting the litany of the Virgin. Prayers continued at the altar. She was still motionless, with her eyes closed. Eventually she stirred, sat up, and patted the stretcher until she found the Franciscan habit. With the help of the priests she put on the habit, struggled out of the stretcher to touch her lips to the hands of the image and the hands of each of the priests. She kissed her mother and husband and sat down on the stretcher, looking intently at the image of the Virgin. Then she indicated that she and her husband had made a solemn vow that needed to be affirmed before the bishop in Guadalajara, and that she wanted to be taken to the Franciscan church to pray before the statue of Jesus and the consecrated Host deposited there. She was no longer speaking, but gestured in a way that made it known that she had received divine instruction not to speak again until she was in the presence of the bishop. The priests said they feared she would exhaust herself and resolved to carry her back to her mother's house, but she gave signs that she must keep vigil at the image of Jesus and, with her husband, reaffirm her vow there. Finally, at about five in the afternoon they carried her home.

On February 22, with his sister on the road to recovery, ecclesiastical judge Larralde certified the depositions of the clergymen who witnessed these events and passed the file to the governor and captain general of the province of the Nuevo Reino de León for his review and remission to the bishop in Guadalajara. Governor Pedro de Barrio Junco, in the presence of the municipal officers of Monterrey, proceeded to summarize events as reported by the witnesses, adding that he had seen Doña María Francisca arise from the stretcher with little help, clear-eyed and with a strong purpose.

The next document in the file is dated March 29 in the bishop's offices in Guadalajara. The file and petition by Doña María Francisca and her husband had been received, and the bishop now appointed three members of the cathedral chapter and a local Jesuit to advise him in the matter. The four reported back on April 7 that there were not sufficient grounds to declare this recovery a miracle or to believe that the Virgin Mary had spoken to the sick woman. Therefore it was most probable that the recovery was natural and Doña María Francisca's vows were not binding. They recommended that the vows be commuted and dispensation be granted. The pilgrimage to Tepeyac, they thought, could do her considerable harm in her weakened condition, but that it was appropriate to show thanks for her recovery in some other way. Whether miraculous or not, it was certainly special, they said. They recommended spiritual exercises, perhaps one or two communions a month for six months or a year, and a charitable gift that the bishop might recommend.

The final document in the file is Bishop Fray Francisco de San Buenaventura Martines de Texada's judgment, dated April 15, 1758. He was more inclined to view Doña María Francisca's recovery as miraculous, describing the episode as a case of a woman of faith gravely ill without hope of recovery, *privada de sentidos* (rendered senseless) for thirty-six days. He concluded, however, that she was "not perfectly in control of her judgment" when she made her vows to the Virgin.[25] Therefore the couple was not bound to the promise of perpetual chastity, and he commuted the promised visit to the shrine of Our Lady of Guadalupe to a donation of five hundred pesos to the building fund of the parish church of Monterrey. In addition, Doña María Francisca was to sponsor a mass for Our Lady of Guadalupe at whatever altar or chapel the parish church might have dedicated to her, to keep vigil there all that day, and for her husband to wear a Franciscan habit over his usual clothing whenever he went to church for the next two years.

Discussion

Except in the cover letter, Doña María Francisca did not speak for herself in the formal record, nor did her mother, Doña Josepha Francisca, but they were leading actors in this provincial drama of illness, faith, healing, salvation, and doubt. They were among those elite laywomen with the time, resources, and inclination to cultivate their spirituality and the well-being of their immortal souls through prayer, frequent confession and communion, good works, and other pious activities. Doña Josepha Francisca set the tone as *mayordoma* of the church fabric in her parish, as mother of one of the city's leading priests, and as the backstage manager of events described in the record. Whether or not the activity of leading officials during Doña María Francisca's prolonged travail should be seen in light of I. M. Lewis's reading of women's possession cults as protests against the dominant sex,[26] she and her mother certainly kept prominent men of the city busy attending to their wishes and instructions. Her husband repeatedly acquiesced in her desire for a celibate life for both of them and her request that he wear a Franciscan habit. Leading priests of the city attended the sickbed in shifts for weeks on end. They responded with alacrity to her mother's urgent request that they come in procession with the miraculous statue of the Virgin. Later they would come again to carry her to the parish church and Franciscan convent and witness her devotions. Doña María Francisca's refusal, on instruction from the Virgin Mary, to speak except to the bishop of Guadalajara left the men to interpret her gestures about what needed to be done next. They also prepared the substantial dossier of notarized depositions and other information that was sent to the bishop for his review and disposition. Despite the men's authority, she and her mother did much to shape the course of events, at least up to the time the case was remitted to the bishop.

The result of the bishop's review, which completes this written record, seems prudent and politic more than inspired. He and his advisers were divided about whether Doña María Francisca's recovery was miraculous, but they agreed that she should not be required to keep her extravagant promises to the Virgin. In place of the arduous pilgrimage to the shrine of Our Lady of Guadalupe and withdrawal into a nun's life of chastity and seclusion, the bishop prescribed a charitable donation to the parish building fund and some light spiritual exercises. The most interested parties in the spiritual question—Doña María Francisca, her husband, Doña Josepha Francisca, and the bishop—apparently got what they wanted at this late stage of the episode. Doña María Francisca was released from her most rigorous vows, her conscience assuaged. Her husband, an important military and political figure in the province, was released from vows that would have altered his life drastically, and to which he had acceded only reluctantly while his wife was seriously ill. For the bishop, excessive spiritual exuberance of distant and important women of his flock was calmed or at least removed to the privacy of their home, and leading citizens of Monterrey reaffirmed his Tridentine authority to mediate between church members and the divine in a time when that authority was challenged.

Why did the stirring recovery of this pious member of a leading local family fail to become one of the canonical miracles of Our Lady of the Walnut Tree, a statue still famous for miraculous cures, now known as Our Lady of the Oak Tree, the perpetual patroness of the city of Monterrey? I don't know.[27] The combination of circumstances in play here may have been indispensable to the outcome. Lack of official sanction and promotion, and the bishop's evident good sense, obviously were important. While he seemed to regard Doña María Francisca's recovery as miraculous, his advisers were convinced otherwise and he did not press the matter. Miracle stories were not so eagerly or universally celebrated and promoted in the late eighteenth century as they had been in the seventeenth century. Ecclesiastical officials in New Spain were more cautious about spreading the news and thereby courting unwanted attention and derision by Bourbon officials who were beginning to press a more limited public role on the church. Moves by mid-eighteenth-century European states at home and abroad toward a more regalist, Erastian church and a more restrained, parsimonious, and decorous spirituality may have influenced the judgment of the bishop and his advisers. So, too, the growing skepticism and empiricism of the time may have disposed the bishop's advisers against Doña María Francisca's recovery as miraculous. (The experts were especially doubtful of her claim to have received instructions from the Virgin.) There was no decisive time of disenchantment in Mexico—as Hartmut Lehmann posits for Germany during the great famine of the early 1770s when, for the first time, a major disaster was not widely seen as the result of God's wrath—but a shift was apparent in small, mostly official ways, including cemetery reforms, wills, and more rigorous standards for judging purported miracles.[28]

Even more decisive for this story's absence from the annals of the miraculous in Nuevo León may have been the nature of Doña María Francisca's recovery and her second thoughts about the promises she made to the Virgin. Her recovery was not sudden and complete (as miracle cures were expected to be), her vacillation over the promises she made—emphatically, on three occasions—and her declared fits of fear or temporary insanity also were not very good material for an edifying miracle story. Change this one fact and I think her recovery would have become an exemplary miracle: if she had kept her promise to take the veil (or perhaps even if she had expired after she recovered consciousness the second time and was able to prepare a good death and make her pronouncement to the people of Monterrey[29]), her story might well have gained favor no matter what royal authorities or the bishop and his advisers intended. Her ringing challenge to the tepid faith of the people of Monterrey might then have echoed for a good, long time among the faithful and stirred the local Franciscans (to whom the two women, both of them named for St. Francis, felt a special attachment) to undertake the kind of revivalist mission that their order's colleges farther south—in Zacatecas, Pachuca, Querétaro, and Mexico City—were known for during the eighteenth century. The *voz pública y fama*—popular opinion and reputation—that authors of devotional histories of shrines and miraculous images invoked to prove the veracity of miracles when they lacked other evidence was crucial to the fame of a shrine.[30] Clerical and lay promoters of shrines and miracle stories might encourage and shape the canon of miracles, but miracles had to seem true and right to many devotees if they were to have much staying power.[31] How active public acceptance of particular shrines, images, and miracles was achieved is another elusive story, but Doña María Francisca's salvo to the people of Monterrey without the promised sacrifice would not have met the test of right and fitting.

Coda

"Sometimes the evidence available in the surviving records of the past will satisfactorily sustain two or more divergent yet credible conclusions about what went on in the past," wrote J. H. Hexter.[32] In this episode of Doña María Francisca's illness and recovery, not to mention the whole subject of miracles, more than one line of interpretation appears to be credible, and mysteries remain. Readers will have their own ideas about this, but here are three to start with. (1) I may have overplayed the two women's roles in shaping the events (although Doña María Francisca's dramatization of her alliance with the Madonna and her very public performances add credibility to it). The priests and other dignitaries of Monterrey, especially her brother the ecclesiastical judge, may well have been full partners with the women in shaping the events—not directed by them as much as working together with them, deciding more or less spontaneously what would come next in this dire, prolonged emergency. Were Doña María Francisca and her mother more afraid than manipulative when she was in the throes of her illness? Were they fixed on the imperative of a good death or bargaining with the divine for her recovery, more than either afraid or manipulative? The shift from her ringing, reiterated vows to doubt about whether she had to fulfill them suggests a change of heart by Doña María Francisca, if not more complex, contradictory feelings from the start. Perhaps the bishop was right in his assessment of her state of mind, and perhaps the priests in Monterrey and Guadalajara were more in control of the events than I suggest here. (2) Perhaps, too, the deliberations at the bishop's court and the failure of Doña María Francisca's cure to rise to the level of a miracle has less to do with disenchantment by anyone in the late eighteenth century than with earnest doubts by all concerned—including the voz pública—about whether she had, in fact, approached the divine in the right ways, in the right frame of mind. And (3), whether the dignitaries and her husband regarded the early events of this episode as an especially delicate time of inversion of gendered social hierarchies in which the sacred was spilling out in unwanted directions, and acted accordingly, is another imponderable. The fact that Doña María Francisca was *in extremis*, that she and her mother were notably faithful (if perhaps pushy) church members calling on the priests to vigorously exercise their institutional and liturgical authority, and that the distinguished men mobilized around her in Monterrey were relatives, friends, and spiritual advisers of the family leads me to doubt that they regarded the unusual demands of her travail as a world turning upside down. However, it is a curious fact that her husband does not speak for himself in the formal proceedings, although the bishop hints at a secret communication and the husband's reluctance to fulfill the vows Doña María Francisca insisted on during her illness.

Document

[p. 1] Summary investigation concerning the marvel that Our Lady of the Walnut Tree worked for Doña María Francisca Larralde, wife of Sergeant Major Don Antonio Urresti, residents of this city of Monterrey, witnessed and written down by Joseph Ygnacio Treviño, notary public of this aforementioned city (1758).

[*Editor's note:* This record of inquiry into events, religious convictions, and doubts associated with the surprising recovery and promises made by Doña María Francisca Larralde who was mortally ill in Monterrey, Nuevo León, in the late 1750s came to light recently in a collection of miscellaneous Mexican records in the Bancroft Library at the University of California, Berkeley. Consisting of twenty-eight leaves of unstamped paper filled with script on both sides of most leaves (which I have treated as pages and noted in the translation), it apparently was filed in the cathedral archive of Guadalajara after the matter was considered and settled by the bishop there. Following a title page composed by Joseph Ignacio Treviño, notary public of Monterrey, who recorded and witnessed all the testimony taken there, the first document is an undated petition to the Bishop of Guadalajara by the married couple, Don Antonio Urresti and Doña María Francisca Larralde, followed by the bishop's acknowledgment of receipt on March 29, 1758, and his order that the record of investigation be reviewed. The bulk of the dossier consists of depositions taken in Monterrey at two stages between January 19 and February 22, 1758, by priests who witnessed the events of Doña María Francisca's illness and recovery. They are open-ended, rather than responding to a set of questions, and they vary enough to appear less rehearsed or guided than is usual in colonial judicial proceedings, whether ecclesiastical, criminal, or civil. The case concludes with these original records being forwarded to the Bishop of Guadalajara on

February 23, and his judgment on April 15 after consulting a panel of experts in theology. Toward the end of the record, the case is summarized four times: by the notary public in Monterrey; by or on behalf of the governor and other residents of Monterrey; by the experts in theology; and by the bishop. These summaries of the depositions inevitably are selective, and occasionally embellish a point not found in the testimony. They are interesting for what is left out as well as what is included.

This is a full translation except for the notary's repetitive opening words as he deposed the witnesses. I include his opening for the first deposition, by Don Bartholomé Molano, to suggest the formula he followed, but have omitted it for the others. A strictly literal translation of this document would be difficult to manage, both for the translator and the reader. The depositions and other legal proceedings appear as if they were delivered in a single breath, without periods or punctuation other than an occasional stray comma, random accents, and unusual capitalization of nouns and verb forms. I have broken the text into sentences, added accents to names, where needed, reverted to modern usage for capitalization unless it seems that the author capitalized for emphasis, and I have tried to give a clear sense of the occasional words and phrases for which there is no straightforward literal translation. An occasional word is added in brackets to clarify a particular context, but I have tried not to make too clear what is not perfectly clear in the original Spanish.]

[p. 2]   Most Illustrious and Most Reverend Sir

Don Antonio de Urresti, Sergeant Major of his majesty's (may God protect him) militia companies of the New Kingdom of León and Doña María Francisca de Larralde, legitimate spouses and residents of the city of Monterrey, prostrate before Your Most Illustrious Lordship, we declare the following. I, said Doña María Francisca, having been gravely ill, as is evident from the proceedings presented to you here, moved by the fear of death, or not being altogether in my right mind because of the severity of the illness, made the vows I am making known to Your Most Illustrious Lordship, to which I, Don Antonio, gave my consent. And [p. 3] being unsure whether they are binding, not knowing whether the illness was natural or preternatural and my recovery miraculous, we appeal to Your Most Illustrious Lordship's piety as our pastor to guide us, resolving the qualms our consciences are suffering. And should the recovery be deemed miraculous and the vows binding, or not being so, if we are still obliged to fulfill some duty, may Your Most Illustrious Lordship be so good as to either declare the vows null and void or, if they are valid in full or in part, commute them or excuse them. We are ready to fulfill the penance you may prescribe in their place.

Therefore, we beg and entreat Your Most Illustrious Lordship to do as we request here, in which we will receive mercy and what is necessary, etcetera.

Doña María Francisca de Larralde and Antonio de Urresti.
[original signatures]

Guadalajara, March 29, 1758

This file having been presented today to Señor Don Fray Francisco de San [p. 4] Buenaventura Martines de Texada, Bishop of Guadalajara, he decreed that proceedings in the matter be undertaken. And so he provided, ordered, and signed.

[rubric of the bishop]
Before me, Joseph Antonio Sánchez de Lara, notary

[p. 5 blank]

[p. 6]   Monterrey, January 19, 1758

An event occurred on the thirteenth day of the present month, between eleven and twelve in the morning, after the sovereign image of Most Holy Mary, Our Lady, which represents the mystery of the Expectation[1] and is commonly called Our Lady of the Walnut Tree and is venerated in the parish church of this city of Monterrey, was taken to the home of Señora Doña Josepha Francisca Cantú del Río y la Cerda, widow of General Don Francisco Ygnacio Larralde. Doña María Francisca de Larralde (daughter of the aforementioned Doña Josepha and wife of Sergeant Major Don Antonio de Urresti, all of them residents of this city) was bedridden with a prolonged illness. The circumstances of the illness were noteworthy because there was every sign that she was nearly dead, in the estimation of all who saw her, including the ecclesiastical judge of the jurisdiction and other priests of this city who expected only to help the sick woman in her last hour. They had been present for a full thirty days since there were signs of imminent death throughout this period and she had not been able to eat. After the aforementioned image of Most Holy Mary of the Walnut Tree had been placed at the foot of the sick woman's bed for a short time that thirteenth of January, adorned with a bracelet of pearls Doña

María Francisca had ordered given to the sovereign image during
the course of her illness, [p. 7] she surprisingly burst out in speech,
joining her hands together and raising her head in praise of the Blessed
Sacrament and the sweetest names of Jesus and Mary. Then calling her
brother's name—who is also the ecclesiastical judge—and the names
of the parish priest of the said city, Bachiller Don Bartholomé Molano,
the Reverend Father President of this [Franciscan] convent, Fray
Miguel de la Portilla, and the other priests to bear witness. And they
heard her refer to the benefits our Lord God had bestowed upon her
in His infinite mercy through the intercession of Most Holy Mary in
her image of the Expectation and here named Our Lady of the Walnut
Tree. Therefore, and so that the event is memorialized in heaven and
to honor Most Holy Mary and the particular veneration of her image
of Our Lady of the Walnut Tree on earth, a summary inquiry with
the honorable parish priest and the other priests mentioned shall
be undertaken into all that happened without omitting any detail,
for all of them are notable, so that Don Francisco Antonio Larralde,
ecclesiastical judge of this capital city and other districts, may decide
what is appropriate in his judgment. And so he decreed and ordered,
before the present notary public, who bears witness.

Bachiller Francisco Antonio Larralde [signature]
Before me, Joseph Ignacio Treviño

[p. 8]

In this city of Monterrey, January 20, 1758, I, the present notary
public, by virtue of the preceding order, went to the home of Señor
Licenciado[2] Don Bartholomé Molano, beneficed parish priest of this
capital, who is known to me. I informed him of the ecclesiastical
judge's order, then took his oath, which he swore as a priest, hand over
his heart.[3] In this way he promised to tell the truth in this matter as far
as he knew and understood it. And he said that in the whole time of
the prolonged illness suffered by Doña María Francisca Larralde, he
personally attended her for thirty-six days in a row without
interruption, from the first day, holding fast to his obligation as pastor
to help her have a good death, since, to his knowledge, no one held out
hope that she would live. And in fact he was there to help her on most
of these days up until the first day of this month. That day, at about
eight in the evening, he was trying to exhort her and move her to
contrition even though she seemed senseless. To see whether she could
give some sign of consciousness, he told her to squeeze his hand, and
she did so. The witness was surprised and called out to the

ecclesiastical judge and the mother to come see this marvelous turn of events. Reverend Father Fray Miguel de la Portilla, president of the convent of Our Father St. Francis of this city was also present, along with Bachiller Don Juan Antonio Garzía, lieutenant pastor of the Valle de Salinas parish, and various other people living in the patient's house. Before all of them she gave various vivid signs of her desire to dedicate various pious works to the sacred images of [p. 9] Jesús Nazareno[4] which is venerated in the church of said convent, and Our Lady Most Holy Mary with the title of Our Lady of the Walnut Tree which is venerated in the parish church of this city, as well as to various impoverished people of the place, which she wished to have recorded in writing so as not to risk any defect, making signs that it should be read to her. And God allowed her at that moment to add the names of the poor to whom she meant to leave some alms. After this, she indicated that her husband, Don Antonio Urresti, Sergeant Major of this kingdom, be called to her side. In the presence of everyone there she indicated that she was asking him to wear a [Franciscan] habit next to his skin should she recover her health, which he agreed to. She immediately made a sign that he should move away from her bed and she proceeded to call all the members of the household and took leave of each one, everyone present being enthralled, thinking that this was her act of taking leave of this life for the other life, which was a consolation to one and all, even more so when she made it clear that she wished to receive the Blessed Sacrament. At that point the said witness proposed to her that she should search her conscience to see whether she had something to confess in order to receive such a supreme benefit. She responded that she had done so. Then he asked if she could ingest the Host without unseemly convulsions since for many days she had been expelling corrupted blood from her body through her mouth without being able to hold down any food, she responded [p. 10] that, yes, she could receive the sacrament. The witness required her to eat something as a test to see if she would regurgitate it and be unable to receive the sacrament. By signs she asked for a little cup of chocolate, which the witness administered, and knowing her great desire to receive His Majesty, that it be given to her, he asked a second time whether she had anything to confess, to which she responded by signs that there was nothing weighing on her mind, whereupon the Host was brought forward, which she received after affirming the mysteries of Our Holy Catholic Faith with great understanding and seemingly true contrition. Some time passed in order to determine whether, because of her great weakness, she might not have been able to consume the Host by herself, she showed that she had by opening her mouth so all could see that not even a particle remained on her tongue. Shortly thereafter, at the urging of the witness and the ecclesiastical judge she ate a little to show there was no doubt that any particle of the sacramental matter was exposed to indecency. The witness swears that this was the only food the patient consumed during all the time he attended her bedside except for a little water she occasionally requested, and the broth that was given to her which did not amount to even a cupful because she was not able to swallow anything. All of these developments lasted from nine [p. 11] in the evening to three in the morning, at which time she fell back into her nearly unconscious state with every sign of being about to die, about which more will be said later and which was evident to all concerned. She was like a dead body from that day until the thirteenth of the present month and year when her mother advised this witness that it had been the wish and intention of her daughter to prostrate herself at the feet of the sovereign image of Our Lady of the Walnut Tree in the parish church and suggested she be taken there. Considering her great weakness and lack of stamina at present, not to mention her nearly unconscious state, this witness and the ecclesiastical judge decided it would be better to bring the sovereign image to the sick woman's house, which was done with the proper decency and assistance of the priests who reside in this city, protected by a *pallium* (liturgical canopy) and *pluvial* (officiating cope), chanting the Litany of the Virgin of Our Lady until they reached the house. The sovereign image was placed at the head of sick woman's bed for a while and then on a decent altar that had been prepared for the purpose. Once this was done, the witness retired to his house, it being about noon. He was eating his meal when Bachiller Don Buenaventura de la Garza, lieutenant pastor of this city arrived in a startled state saying that the sick woman was calling the pastor in a loud voice. He found her so resolved in these agitated utterances, and surmising that she was calling him to help her in her last hour, [p. 12] his lieutenant said to him, "Come, Señor Cura, to witness a miracle and great marvel that my Lady of the Walnut Tree had done with this cadaver." The witness confirmed it, seeing the patient's earlier pledge of a bracelet of costly pearls placed on the virgin body of the Lady immediately reciprocated, His Majesty granting her health and speech so that she could declare what to all is evident, her first utterances being in praise of the Most Blessed Sacrament and of the sweetest names of Jesus, Mary, and Joseph, asking everyone in attendance, at the peal of the church bells whose tongues cried aloud with the pleasure caused by this extraordinary moment and because their clamor was moved by a very special thing, to urge that the people practice a very special devotion to Our Lady of the Walnut Tree, reserving Saturday to honor His Majesty, for by her intercession [Mary's, through the image of Our Lady of the Walnut Tree] she was restored to life. She also declared in a strong voice that one of the principal reasons why this city was in abject decline was the lack of devotion and veneration to this Divine Lady, and that she had been shown that this intercession had liberated her from the flames of the living and the dead for having failed to follow her vocation since, from the time she was a girl, it was her intention and will to remain chaste and become a spouse of Jesus Christ in a convent [p. 13], which she did not do because her parents did not put at her disposal the means to carry out His saintly purpose, perhaps because she never made her calling known to them. Now she did so on the very day her speech and consciousness returned, when, with the parish priest and other persons already named as witnesses, she asked her husband to allow her to be chaste from then on and let her go to visit my Lady of Guadalupe, whose shrine is located near Mexico City, and walk the last three leagues to that holy house, as he had promised in the state she was in during her long unconsciousness. All of this he agreed to, considering that it was for the good of her soul and in the service of God. Everything recounted here is the sworn truth, which the witness affirms, ratifies and signs before me, to which I attest.

Bartholomé Molano [signature]
Before me, Don José Ignacio Treviño, notary public

In the city of Monterrey, January 21, 1758 . . . [p. 14] the Very Reverend Father Fray Miguel de la Portilla, Franciscan of the Regular Observance, retired most worthy president of the convent . . . testified that from December 16 of last year to January 13 of the present year, he has attended Doña María Francisca Larralde, wife of Sergeant Major Don Antonio Urresti in her mortal illness. During this time he has not seen her take nourishment of any kind except for the night of January 1 when, by very vivid signs, she requested a cup of chocolate so that those in attendance might see that she would be able to receive Holy Communion, and she anxiously and with particular signs made various provisions, the first being to donate, with her husband's consent (whom she called to her side) her bracelet of [p. 15] fine pearls from the Orient with their golden clasps to Our Lady of the Walnut Tree which is venerated in the parish church of this capital city; donating also to the sovereign image of the Nazarene which is venerated in the church of this [Franciscan] convent a golden reliquary

with its golden palm frond of martyrdom; also some of her clothing to
three destitute women of this place; also a certain legacy to Our Lady
of Carmen for an annual sung mass, and a certain offering to the souls
in Purgatory, which the steward of this devotion shall administer. She
also requested that she be buried not in the chapel of the parish church
built at the expense of her parents, but in the church of the Franciscan
convent at the foot of the altar of Jesus. By the same signs she also
asked to be dressed for burial in the seraphic habit of my already
mentioned Father [St. Francis], putting her hands together to plead
for this provision for the love of God, and that her body be placed in
the ground. After this, the sacred viaticum[5] was administered to her
by the hand of the parish priest of this city which she took with the
necessary decency, giving signs of contrition, to the great consolation
of those in attendance, who were admiring and totally edified, for
in order to demonstrate that she had swallowed the Host, displayed
her mouth and tongue. Then she called forward her husband and
members of the household to say goodbye, [p. 16] asking all of them
with signs to pardon her. On the thirteenth of the current month
at about 2:00 a.m. she slipped back into her state of utter lethargy.
That day the ecclesiastical judge of the aforementioned parish priest
decided to bring the sovereign image of Our Lady of the Walnut Tree
to the home of the sick woman who was so passionate about this cult.
After having placed the image on an altar that was prepared by her
mother, in a very appropriate manner for the purpose in the bedroom
of the sick woman, the mother began to place the bracelet of pearls on
the statue of the Most Holy Virgin, and while she was doing so, the
witness noticed that the patient began to make very definite physical
signs, which Bachiller Don Buenaventura de la Garza, who was
standing with him, also noticed. And shortly after the pearls had been
put in place, between twelve and one o'clock in the afternoon of the
aforementioned day, the witness was helping her in her last agonies,
the vicario[6] approached the bedside and soon the moribund patient
opened her eyes and burst out in a loud voice praising the Eucharist
and Most Holy Mary of Sorrows and the sweetest name of Jesus,
calling by their names the ecclesiastical judge, the parish priest, and
the present witness and other priests to [p. 17] come see the prodigious
development worked for her by God through the intercession of Our
Lady of the Walnut Tree, for she found herself restored to life when
she had seemed to be a cadaver. And while the parish priest was
being summoned from his home, she called also for her husband, Don
Antonio de Urresti, who was astonished that she had revived, as was
the parish priest. In the presence of the aforementioned priests, the

patient expressed herself in the following manner, in a clear voice, with great firmness: that the parish priest had united them in the sacrament of holy matrimony, which the ecclesiastical judge and the other priests present had witnessed; now, taking her husband's hand, she asked that the two of them remain chaste for the rest of their lives, that he agree (1) to wear next to his skin the sainted habit of our seraphic Father (St. Francis) for a period of two years and go (with her), (2) to visit the holy temple of Our Lady of Guadalupe near Mexico City and would make the last three leagues of the pilgrimage on foot, and (3) to make it known to everyone how pleasing it was to God Our Lord that Catholics reserve Saturdays to honor Our Most Holy [p. 18] Mother (This nearly devastated city pays a price for its tepid devotion to her), to which he agreed. And she said that God had freed her from the flames of the living and dead by the intercession of Our Lady of the Walnut Tree and St. Joseph for having erred in her vocation. As an eyewitness, the Reverend Father affirms his account of what happened; and having heard it read to him for start to finish, he ratified it under oath and signed it before me, to which I attest.

Fray Miguel de la Portilla [signature]
Before me, José Ignacio Treviño, public notary

In the city of Our Lady of Monterrey on January 22, 1758 . . . Señor Licenciado Don Juan Báez Treviño, commissary of the Apostolic and Royal Tribunal of the Crusade, notary of the Holy Office of the Inquisition of this kingdom, and resident of this capital, resident priest of this diocese [p. 19] . . . said that, despite his chronic illnesses, since December 17 of last year he had been going to the home of Doña Josepha Francisca Cantú del Río y la Cerda, widow of General Don Francisco Ygnacio Larralde, may he rest in peace, because her daughter, Doña María Francisca Larralde was gravely ill, and as a priest he was there to do whatever he could for the good of her soul. And finding her, in fact, without hope of recovery in this life, he exhorted her repeatedly to attend to her soul and moved her to contrition because she seemed to be in the last throes of her suffering, especially since she had taken no nourishment at all until the night of the first day of this month when she drank a cup of chocolate. He was not there to witness this event, but the next day, Fathers Fray Miguel de la Portilla, Don Bartholomé Molano, parish priest of this city, and Don Juan Antonio García, assistant pastor of Salinas told him so, adding that she had received the *viaticum* from the hand of the parish priest, and made signs that amounted to a virtual testamentary

disposition, providing that her burial should be in the convent of the
Franciscans of this capital even though a place was reserved in the
parish church. She also made known certain vows that before
[p. 20] her death her husband Don Antonio de Urresti, Sergeant Major
of this kingdom, as her legitimate spouse, would fulfill, including
the donation of her bracelet of fine pearls, which was done on the
thirteenth of this present month of January when, in his presence,
they were placed on the image of Our Lady of the Walnut Tree which
is venerated in this parish church, when their most divine Lady was
brought to the home of the sick woman, brought by the priests with
every decency observed, hoping that her divine intervention would be
forthcoming, if fitting, in her return to health. And so it happened, as
it seemed to all, the most singular marvel of the restoration of speech
and movement of her hands, which she had not moved for many
days, and her eyes, which she had not opened for a long time during
her prodigious suffering. All of this happened on the aforementioned
thirteenth day, and it is the truth, he swears, affirms, and ratifies. And
he signed it before me, to which I attest.

Juan Báez Treviño [signature]
Before me, José Ignacio Treviño, public notary

    In the city of Monterrey on January 22, 1758 [p. 21] . . . Licenciado
Don Luis Buenaventura de la Garza, resident priest of this diocese,
assistant pastor of this capital . . . testified that it is common knowledge
that Doña María Francisca Larralde, wife of the Sergeant Major of
this kingdom has suffered a long illness that has seemed fatal to
everyone, since for over thirty days she was almost moribund and
without nourishment, expelling only fetid blood from her mouth.
Then, at night on the first day of the present month she came out of
her lethargy, drank a cup of chocolate and, by efficacious signs, asked
that she be given communion in the viaticum, which was administered
to her by the parish priest of this capital. After this, she proceeded to
provide for her burial and make various pious vows with the express
consent of her husband, who was summoned by the same gestures in
order to express her wishes to him as well as take leave of this mortal
life, which she also did with all the members of her household. Then
she fell back into her state of stupor until the thirteenth of the current
month when the ecclesiastical judge and the parish priest decided to
bring [p. 22] from the parish church to the home of the sick woman the
sovereign image of Our Lady of the Walnut Tree which is venerated
in the aforementioned church, and which was transported with the

appropriate decency, under a pallium and pluvial, accompanied by
the priests who reside in this city. The aforementioned Lady was
placed on a decent altar prepared for her in the bedroom of the sick
woman, facing her bed. At about twelve o'clock noon the witness saw
the bracelet of [p. 15] fine pearls from the Orient, which Doña María
Francisca had placed on the image by Señora Doña Josepha Francisca
Cantú, legitimate mother of the aforementioned Doña María Francisca,
by order of her husband, Don Antonio de Urresti. The witness was
next to the Reverend Father President of the convent of this city,
urging the patient to attend to her soul, and a short time later he
observed that she moved her hands and opened her eyes, and began
to make extraordinary utterances, praising the Blessed Sacrament and
the sweetest names of Jesus, Mary, and Joseph, declaring that by the
intercession of Our Lady of the Walnut Tree she had been restored to
this mortal life from the eternal one, for she thought she was dead.
And this witness saw that she called by name the ecclesiastical judge,
the Reverend Father President, and the parish priest. She also called
for Don Antonio de Urresti and, taking his hand, asked him to remain
chaste for the rest of his life and wear next to his skin for two years
[p. 23] the habit of Our Father St. Francis, and go with her to visit Our
Lady of Guadalupe in Mexico City and travel the last three leagues
there on foot. The witness noted that Doña María knew this thirteenth
day was a Friday, the eve of the feast of the sweetest name of Jesus
[the words Mary and Joseph are crossed out], even though she had
been senseless for so many days. The witness swears that what he has
declared is true, which he affirms and ratifies. And he signed it before
me, to which I attest.

Luis Buenaventura de la Garza [signature]
Before me, José Ignacio Treviño, notary public

Monterrey, February 17, 1758

At about 11:30 in the morning of this day, Doña María Francisca
Larralde, accompanied by Sergeant Major of this kingdom Don
Antonio de [p. 24] Urresti, her legitimate husband, is in the church of
Our Father St. Francis of this city, in the presbytery facing the altar of
the image of the Nazarene, which is venerated in this church. She was
carried at about 10:00 to the parish church of said city in a moribund
state to visit the sovereign image of Our Lady of the Walnut Tree, after
the priests in attendance and the leading citizens of this capital had
sung the litany. At that point it was seen that the lady in question was

restored to complete health and judgment, after having been in death
throes for about ten days running, as is well known. With quite a bit of
strength, with the aid of the priests, she was raised to her feet to touch
the hands of the sovereign image with her mouth, and she gave a sign
that the aforementioned priests come up to her, and she touched the
hands of each one of them with her mouth. After this, she gave signs
that she wanted to be carried to this said church in order to adore
the Blessed Sacrament, since at that time the provision of consecrated
bread was there, and to visit the image of Jesus. After everyone present
prayed at the request of Doña María Francisca, she indicated that she
and her aforementioned husband had celebrated a religious vow and
it needed to be confirmed before the Most Illustrious and Reverend
Lord Bishop of this diocese (my Lord), that, by divine command, only
in his presence would she be able to speak again, may it please and
bring greater honor and glory to God Our Lord, and veneration of
Most Holy Mary, Our Lady, particularly in this new kingdom of León
[p. 25] in her aforementioned image of the Walnut Tree. Bachiller Don
Francisco Antonio Larralde, vicar ecclesiastical judge said that it should
be ordered, and he so ordered, that these proceedings be set down in
writing, recognizing that the said Doña María requested it, and the
present notary receive summary testimony about the matter from the
parish priest of this capital and other priests who were present, as
well as the Reverend Father President of this convent, after which an
appropriate order will be given. And so it was decreed, before me, to
which I attest.

Bachiller Francisco Antonio Larralde [signature]
Before me, José Ignacio Treviño, public notary

In the city of Our Lady of Monterrey on February 17, 1758, in
compliance with what has been ordered, I, the present notary, went
to the home of Licenciado Don Bartholomé Molano, parish priest by
royal appointment of this capital city. . . . [p. 26] He testified that Doña
María had, indeed, been restored to full speech and consciousness
on the thirteenth of January and remained in this state until the
seventh of the present month when, with great insistence, she called
for the witness to come and confess her, which he did at around ten
or eleven in the morning. She was in full command of her senses and
displayed true signs of Catholic Christianity. At about seven or eight
o'clock that night she returned to her former stupor, with even greater
indications of her imminent death than before, after such a long period
of debility and with little strength to resist. Then today she was carried

to the parish church of this city to prostrate herself at the feet of the miraculous image of Our Lady of the Walnut Tree that is venerated there, in accordance with her longstanding desire. This was done in the presence of all the priests of the city, the Lord Governor and Captain General, and other distinguished persons. She was placed on the platform of the main altar, where the image is kept in its tabernacle for its greater decency and the greater veneration of all the inhabitants. She was prostrate there, [p. 27] like a dead body, while the priests chanted aloud the litany of Our Lady, ending in prayer. At that time a novena to the miraculous image was underway for the purpose of beseeching the Most Holy Majesty to grant what was most agreeable to her and her Most Holy Son. And when the prayer ended she began to move her feet, as if wishing to get up, and, in fact, in a short time she turned and moved toward the altar. The witness and Bachiller Don Joseph Lorenzo Báez Treviño conjectured that a sudden urgency had come over her, perhaps a premonition of death, and they rushed to her. She seemed to be trying to take hold of the habit of Our Father St. Francis, and gave signs for them to put it on her, which they did. Dressed in that habit, she turned her eyes to the miraculous image, and with great yearning and fervor she threw herself toward the image, which she could not reach by herself because of her frailty and weakness. But the assistant parish priest, the witness, and Bachiller Don Joseph Lorenzo Báez Treviño helped her do so. They held her there, resting on tiptoe, reaching for the Miraculous Image, which had been taken down from its tabernacle and [p. 28] placed on the altar as she had requested with gestures. There, with great devotion, she kissed the most holy hands and feet and clothing of the Lady. No longer able to hold herself in this position, they lowered her onto the bed in which she had been carried to the church. There, after praying for some time she gave a sign that she be carried, but the witness, as well as the assistant pastor, were uncertain about where she wanted to go because she indicated only with gestures. The assistant pastor asked her to explain more clearly what she wanted, to which she responded with more gestures that indicated clearly that she could not do so in spoken words under any circumstances until she was in the presence of the Most Illustrious and Most Reverend Lord Bishop of this diocese (my Lord), indicating that this was by a higher command that she not speak until then. Persisting in her gestures, she indicated in particular that they take her to the convent of Our Father St. Francis to visit and give thanks to the miraculous image of the Nazarene. There, after giving thanks to this Divine Image, she indicated that she wished to reiterate before the consecrated Host the vow that this witness described in his previous testimony. To that end she, in the company of her husband and with his permission, renewed the vow, adding the religious vow, [p. 29] if the aforementioned Most Illustrious Lord [the bishop] would allow when she is able to explain the reasons to him, which her husband willingly agreed to. This declaration is the truth, under oath, which the witness affirms and ratifies, and which he signed before me, to which I attest.

Bartholomé Molano [signature]
Before me, José Ignacio Treviño, notary public

In the city of Monterrey, February 20, 1758 . . . Most Reverend Father Fray Miguel de la Portilla of the Observant branch, retired prior and most meritorious president of said convent . . . testified that when he left the convent to visit the home of Doña María Larralde, whom he had left the previously night in extremely grave danger of dying, he found [p. 30] the house empty because the members of the household and other respectable people had gone to the parish church of this city to take her to the Most Holy Image of Our Lady of the Walnut Tree which is kept on the main altar. Realizing where they were, the witness went to the aforementioned church and found the sick woman in a moribund state in front of the altar and all the priests and other people there chanting the litany of Our Lady. Once they finished and an appropriate prayer was offered by the parish priest, they prayed a novena to this advocation of Our Lady, which the family had already begun. Once this was finished, the church fell silent, everyone silently making his or her appeal to God Our Lord and the Most Holy Virgin. Then, while most people were on their feet, they saw the immobile body move, and with little effort and some quickness sit up and reach for the habit of our seraphic Father St. Francis which had been placed on top of the clothing that covered her. She began to make an effort to put it on, and they came up to help her. With little effort she rose to her feet, extending her hands as if she, the favored, wished to go up and embrace her Divine benefactor. At this, the Governor of this kingdom began to intone the hymn sung in honor of the Eucharist, and the sick woman had one of the priests bring the image down to where she could kiss its hands and give thanks for having received the apparent favor. She also requested with gestures the hands of all the priests present, and she kissed them with great veneration and reverence, doing the same with her mother and husband. Returning to her bed, she sat down and gazed for a while with rapt attention at the Most Holy Virgin. Then by signs she indicated that she wished to be taken to the convent of Our Father St. Francis in order to visit in the church there [p. 31] the sovereign image of Jesus and to adore the Blessed Sacrament, which she did with great devotion. She also made signs to indicate that in the presence of the Most Illustrious and Most Reverend Lord Bishop of this diocese (my Lord) she would speak, but that now she was not able to do so because of divine sanction. And seeing that it was already late, they told her that they would now take her home, to which she gave signs that she did not want to leave yet, that she wished to keep vigil with the image of Jesus, as she did in fact until about four or five in the afternoon. Before the *via crucis* procession began, they carried her, much comforted, to her house. This is an accurate account of what this Reverend Father witnessed, with great admiration, and it is the truth under oath, which he affirms and ratifies. And he signed it before me, to which I attest.

Fray Miguel de la Portilla [signature]
Before me, José Ignacio Treviño, notary public

In the city of Monterrey on February 20, 1758 . . . Licenciado Don Juan Báez Treviño, resident of this capital [p. 32] and resident priest of this diocese, commissary of the Apostolic and Royal Tribunal of the Crusade, notary of the Holy Office of the Inquisition . . . testified that since the thirteenth of last month, when Doña María Francisca Larralde experienced the favor of the Most Holy Virgin Mary, Our Lady of the Walnut Tree and was able to speak and move her hands and eyes as before, he was in communication with her almost every day until the sixth of the present month, at which time he observed no particular change in her health. Then he did not visit her for three days because he was sick. When he passed by the house again to visit her, he learned that since the seventh she had relapsed into her previous state, with even greater signs that she was about to die. She was unable to ingest any food and could not even take water because her throat was swollen. She was in such pain that when she needed to spit, she suffered such anguish, it seemed, that even her hands and arms were convulsed. Watching these signs of anguish caused great sadness. On the fifteenth, the priests who saw her judged that she was suffering the final agonies, and on the seventeenth her husband, Sergeant Major Don Antonio Urresti decided to have her taken to the parish church of this city to be in the presence [p. 33] of the Most Holy Lady. This was done at about ten in the morning. There in the church the litany was intoned with great devotion, and after it and a certain novena that her people were praying finished, the sick woman began to move, turning

her head toward where the Most Holy Virgin was. This was not
particularly surprising to the witness because it seemed to him to be
caused by the illness, as he has said. But a short time later he saw that
she wanted to get up from the bed on which she had been placed and
go up to the Most Holy Image. With help, she got up, making gestures
to indicate that she wished to kiss the garments and hands of the Most
Holy Lady; and when the image was brought down from its tabernacle
and placed on the platform of the main altar, her desire was fulfilled.
Then she gave signs of wishing to kiss the hands of the priests,
which she carried out with great humility. After all these acts she was
carried to the convent of our Father St. Francis, having expressed by
signs her wish to go there. She seemed to give thanks to the image
of the Nazarene in the said convent, and then she adored the Blessed
Sacrament, which was brought out for the purpose. And she seemed
to express that she, in her husband's presence, wanted to take religious
vows before the Most Illustrious and Most Reverend Lord Bishop of
this diocese (my Lord). Under oath he swore that this was the truth,
which he affirmed and ratified. And he signed it in my presence, to
which I attest.

Juan Báez Treviño [signature]
Before me, José Ignacio Treviño, notary public

    In [p. 34] the city of Our Lady of Monterrey on February 21, 1758
. . . the Reverend Father Fray Blas Antonio de Quintanilla, retired
Observant Franciscan and resident of this convent . . . testifies that he
knows it is true that Doña María Francisca Larralde was bedridden,
unable to speak or open her eyes for ten days, and he also knows
that when he attended to her she took no food or water, and that he
has heard from those who were present that when he was not there
everyone feared for her life. And he knows that Doña María was in
this state for a long time and he has been told that through a miracle
of Most Holy Mary, Our Lady in her image of the Walnut Tree which
is venerated in this parish church (which Christian proceedings he
did not personally witness), she was restored to health. He attests that
having left her in the unfortunate state he has described, without hope
of living, he made a journey [p. 35] on the orders of his superiors and
when he returned to this city he found her able to speak and with all of
her mental faculties, which she did not display before. And believing,
as he firmly believes, that the merits of Most Holy Mary, Our Lady
with the highest honor of Mother of God, to which she was elevated,
are sufficient for God Our Lord to shower the treasures of His Divine

omnipotence even in the most prodigious and rare marvels on His most miserable and sinful children such as this witness. Therefore, with all certainty and Christian faith he helped the mourners of the said Doña María Larralde to seek the protection and tutelage of the Most Holy Mary, Our Lady in her image of the Walnut Tree. To this end, on the morning of the seventeenth of the present month he was among the group that went to the parish church and placed the aforementioned Doña María in her bed on the platform of the altar. There the priests in attendance chanted the litany of Our Lady, with response by all of Christ's faithful who were there, followed by a novena in which the devout of her household participated. When this was over, Doña María moved her feet and in short order—about the length of time it takes to pray a Credo [the Apostles' Creed]—her whole body moved as she tried to stand up, to the extent that she arose and reached the niche where the image was placed. Everyone followed, and even the witness helped bring down the image so that she could venerate and kiss it, which she did. And when she was asked to speak she made signs that she would not do so until she could meet with the Most Illustrious and Most Reverend Lord Bishop of this diocese (my Lord). Also with gestures she asked to be taken to our convent to visit the image of the Nazarene, which is venerated there. The witness accompanied them to the entrance of the said church [p. 36], where he retired on important business. He knows no more. And so he declares and affirms that it is his desire that his testimony be given in honor and glory of God Our Lord, Most Holy Mother Mary, Our Lady, and for the greater devotion and veneration of her image of the Walnut Tree. And he signed it before me, to which I attest.

Fray Blas Antonio de Quintanilla [signature]
Before me, José Ignacio Treviño, public notary

In this city of Monterrey on February 21, 1758 . . . Licenciado Don Luis Buenaventura de la Garza . . . assistant pastor of this capital . . . testified that on the seventeenth of this month at about 10:00 a.m., at the request of Sergeant Major Don Antonio Urresti, they carried his legitimate wife, Doña María Francisca Larralde, in her bed to the parish church of this city. For the past ten days it seemed to everyone that she was nearly [p. 37] dead, with no signs of life other than the natural movement of her breathing; and, to the witness's knowledge, during that time she ate or drank nothing at all. The sick woman was lying at the foot of the main altar where the sovereign image of Our Lady of the Walnut Tree was located, and after the priests intoned the litany of Most Holy Mary, Our Lady, the aforementioned president said a prayer, members of her family continued praying a particular novena, and those present made their individual appeals to the sovereign image as protectress of this kingdom that she approach her precious son and that the sick woman have the benefit of whatever might lead to her salvation. Shortly afterward, the witness saw her move her feet, at which point the priests drew near her. Then, in about the time it takes to say the Credo, she sat up on her bed with her eyes closed and patted the bedclothes until she came upon the habit of Our Father St. Francis, which she wanted to put on. They helped her do so, and at that point she opened her eyes and tried to stand up. She did so with little help from those who were there to assist her, indicating that she wanted to kiss the hands of the divine Lady. The image was brought down from its tabernacle and placed on the altar where she kissed it with utter veneration. She also indicated that she wished to kiss the hands of the priests, which she did with complete humility, as she did also with her mother and husband. Then, sitting on the bed, she indicated that she wished to be taken to the church of Our Father St. Francis in this city to visit the image [p. 38] of the Nazarene and the consecrated Host, which at present is being kept there. There she did so, and while in the presbytery of the church, in front of the altar to Jesus, after genuflecting with great devotion, she asked through gestures that all the priests and others present pray to His Divine Majesty and show their adoration for the Blessed Sacrament. When asked why she did not say in words what she wanted to convey, she expressed in signs that she was not to move her tongue until she was with the Most Illustrious and Most Reverend Lord Bishop of this diocese (my Lord), with whom she needed to speak, commanded by Divine Providence. What has been declared here under oath is the truth, which the witness affirms, ratifies, and signs before me, to which I attest.

Luis Buenaventura Garza [signature]
Before me, José Ignacio Treviño, notary public

In the city of Monterrey on February 22, 1758 . . . Licenciado Don Joseph Lorenzo Báez Treviño . . . former assistant pastor of this capital . . . [p. 39] testified that on the seventeenth of the present month at about ten in the morning they took Doña María Francisca Larralde to the parish church of this city in an apparently unconscious state, showing no more sign of life for the past ten days than her breathing. Her husband, the Sergeant Major, accompanied by the most distinguished people of this capital, now placed her at the foot of the altar of Our Lady of the Walnut Tree. After the litany of Our Lady was chanted, a little time passed in which the sixth day of the novena of the Encarnation was prayed. Then Doña María sat up suddenly and even went over to kiss the altar. And, aided by the witness and others, she kissed the hands of the Most Holy Image. Giving signs to the priests, her mother, and her husband with her hands, she asked to submit to them, and she also asked to be taken to the convent of Our Lord St. Francis where she prayed to the Blessed Sacrament and the image of the Nazarene, as did those present, at her request. She declared with clear and intelligible signs that she and her husband were being called by God to the religious life, and she asked her husband that the two of them make a vow before the Blessed Sacrament and the holy image of Jesus, indicating that, with his permission, she would do it and that he should do the same. He agreed on the express condition that this was the command of God. She also made known that the two of them should go to the Most Illustrious and Most Reverend Lord [p. 40] Bishop of this diocese, before whom they would confirm their vow, and he would give her back the use of her tongue. What is declared here under oath is the truth, which the witness affirms, ratifies, and signs in my presence, to which I attest.

Joseph Lorenzo Báez de Treviño [signature]
Before me, José Ignacio Treviño, notary public

Monterrey, February 22, 1758

Having reviewed these proceedings, Bachiller Don Francisco Larralde, ecclesiastical judge [*vicario juez eclesiástico*] of this capital, directs that the notary who has signed them shall certify in the proper manner all that concerns this matter as he understands it. Once it is done, suitable provision will be made. So decreed, in my presence, to which I attest.

Bachiller Francisco Antonio Larralde [signature]
Before me, José Ignacio Treviño, notary public

I, the present public notary of this capital of Our Lady of Monterrey, New Kingdom of León, certify and attest that I am giving true testimony [p. 41] as far as possible that Doña María Francisca Larralde, legitimate wife of the Sergeant Major of this kingdom, Don Antonio de Urresti, was, in everyone's judgment, for thirty-six days running, without hope of surviving her prolonged illness. During that time, as trustworthy witnesses who attended her have told me, she ate nothing until the first day of January of the present year. At that time, at the urging of the parish priest she drank a cup of chocolate, and that night she indicated by signs what her testament should include, leaving various pious works, including the donation of a bracelet of fine Oriental pearls with gold clasps to Our Lady of the Walnut Tree which is venerated in the parish church of this city. She asked for the viaticum, which was administered to her by the parish priest of this said city. After this, she fell back into a senseless state, which lasted without interruption until the thirteenth of the month. At that time, at the request of her family, the ecclesiastical judge and the parish priest decided to bring the Most Holy Lady of the Walnut Tree to her home. It was brought with the appropriate decency and placed on an altar prepared in the bedroom of the aforementioned Doña María, as her husband and mother had arranged. After prostrating themselves and praying before the aforementioned Most Holy Virgin, the bracelet of pearls was placed on the image. Then the sick woman burst out in extraordinary speech, praising the sweetest names of Jesus, Mary, and Joseph, and calling for the ecclesiastical judge, the parish priest, the Reverend Father President of the convent of this city, and other priests who were attending her so that they would bear witness to the marvel that God Our Lord had worked on her through the intercession of Our Lady of the Walnut Tree. She also called for her husband, whom she asked to remain chaste [p. 42] for the rest of his life, to wear next to his skin the seraphic habit of my Father St. Francis for a period of two years, and to visit my Lady of Guadalupe in Mexico City, traveling on foot for the last three leagues of the pilgrimage. It seems to me especially noteworthy that the aforementioned Doña María would recognize at that instant, after so long in a state of lethargy, that it was Friday and the eve of the feast of the Sweetest Name of Jesus. Her recovery continued, as is common knowledge, until the seventh of the present month when, at about seven or eight at night, she returned to her former state of stupor and with even greater signs of being near death. During the ten days that this relapse continued she consumed no nourishment, not even water. At that point, on the seventeenth, her husband decided that she should be taken in her own bed to the parish church of this city to appeal for the intercession of Our Lady. This was done, in the company of the priests, the governor of this kingdom, and other persons of the first rank of this republic. She was placed on the platform of the altar of the sovereign image. After the priests chanted the litany of Our Lady and prayed a certain novena that members of her household had begun,

the aforementioned Doña María began to move, as if she wanted to
sit up. She patted the bedclothes until she touched the habit of our
seraphic Father and tried to put it on. With help, she was able to do
so and to stand up and kiss the altar and the hands of Our Lady with
complete veneration. She gave signs that she wanted the priests, her
mother, and her husband to come forward so that she could do the same
with them, which she did with humility, and asked for their blessing.
She also indicated with gestures that she wanted to be taken [p. 43] to
the convent of our Father St. Francis of this city in order to show her
adoration for the Blessed Sacrament and the sovereign image of the
Nazarene. There she prayed and urged those in attendance to pray. She
declared by signs that God Our Father called her and her husband to
the religious life, and that by divine determination they were to appear
before the Most Illustrious and Most Reverend Lord Bishop of this
diocese (my Lord). Until then she could not speak. So that this may
be recorded in whatever tribunal may be appropriate, I present it in
accordance with the preceding decree, in Monterrey on February 22,
1758, to all of which I attest.

José Ignacio Treviño [signature], notary public

Monterrey, February 23, 1758

In view of what is contained in these latest proceedings, the
requisite letter is to be sent to the court of the governor of this
kingdom requesting that it remit to the governor a certification of these
proceedings, as called for [by the ecclesiastical judge in his decree] on
February 17, in the form used by the said governor and republicans of
this city, and that it be added to the full proceedings and remitted to
the most Illustrious and Most Reverend Lord Bishop of this diocese,
my Lord. The ecclesiastical judge decreed this, to which I attest.

Bachiller Francisco Antonio Larralde [signature]
Before me, José Ignacio Treviño, notary public

[p. 44]

Monterrey, February 23, 1758. The certification remitted to this
[ecclesiastical] court by the governor and captain general of this
kingdom in response to the preceding decree was added to the
proceedings. So that it is registered, I include it among the
proceedings, to which I attest.

José Ignacio Treviño, notary public

[p. 45 blank]

[p. 46]

We—General Don Pedro de Barrio Junco y Espriella, governor
and captain general of this New Kingdom of León, appointed by
His Majesty (May God protect him), Don Joseph Alexandro Muñoz
de Herrera, *regidor* and perpetual provincial *alcalde* of this city, the
honorable members of the republic, Don Antonio Marcos de Cosío,
Don Joseph Joachin de Mier y Noriega, Don Joseph Ortiz de Otteo,
alcaldes ordinarios, and Don Francisco de Rivera, who has also been
an alcalde ordinario of the said city of Monterrey, the residents of
the city Don Juan Ygnacio Verridi, Don Juan Angel Cavallero de los
Olivos, Don Francisco Antonio de Salzedo y Villamill, Don Joachin
Martines Guexardo, also former alcaldes ordinarios and respectable
people, and all the priests, including the vicario and ecclesiastical
judge, Don Francisco Antonio de Larralde, Bachiller Don Bartholomé
Molano, parish priest of this city by appointment of His Majesty,
his assistant Don Buenaventura de la Garza, Bachiller Don Joseph
Lorenzo de Treviño, the Very Reverend Father Guardian Fray
Miguel de la Portilla, and the Observant Franciscan Fray Blas de
Quintanilla, along with many individuals of both sexes and various
stations in society, etcetera—certify, attest, and give true testimony
together and each one of us that we declare to the greater honor and
glory of God and Most Holy Mary, Our Lady, that today Sergeant
Major Don Antonio de Urresti took his wife and conjoined partner
Doña María de Larralde—who had been sick in bed for eleven
days suffering paroxysms and lethargy and could not take food of
any kind or even water or other liquid, without speech, sight, or
consciousness—to offer her into the care of Most Holy Mary whose
image is venerated in this parish church with the advocation of Our
Lady of the Walnut Tree, who appeared in an oak tree in these parts
according to venerable popular opinion. After being placed on her
bed before the altar, and after the litany was chanted by the clergy
and the corresponding prayer made and the continuation of à novena
that members of her family had started, God chose to give the sick
woman courage to sit up, open her eyes and raise her hands to God
and the sovereign image of Most Holy Mary, rising to her feet with a
little help, and with clear and perceptible signs, clear eyes, and fully
conscious, gave thanks for a period of time. With signals she asked to
be seated, and she made known that it was the will of God and Most

Holy Mary that she not speak until she was in the presence of the Most Illustrious Lord Bishop, denying [p. 47] the interpretation of her signs that did not correspond to her wishes, and affirming those that did correspond to her mind and will. Above all, with these signs she asked for the hand of every priest, and she kissed each one reverently. She also asked for the hand of the lady, her mother, and asked her for her blessing, which she received with humility. Calling upon her husband in the same manner and in his presence, she looked at him and recognized him, and asked for his blessing and said goodbye. She seemed to beg his pardon, which was evidenced by the act of kissing his hand. After these actions and fervent silent prayers, she asked to be taken to the convent church of my Father St. Francis. There she demonstrated her adoration for the Blessed Sacrament with fervor, asking that she be taken to the sacristy where she sat down unaided, to keep vigil. So that this prodigious event as we have described it may be recorded for all time for the greater honor and glory of God and greater devotion to the sovereign image of Our Lady which is venerated in the parish church under the advocation of the Walnut Tree, we present this writing and order that it be filed in the archive of this kingdom forever. We sign it today, February 17, 1758, on ordinary paper because no stamped paper is to be found in this province, to which we attest. Don Pedro de Barrio Junco y Espriella, Don Joseph Alexandro Muñoz de Herrera, Don Antonio Marcos de Cosío, Don Joseph Joachin de Mier Noriega, Don Francisco de Rivera y Castro, Don Ignacio Verridi, Don Francisco de Salzedo y Villamil, Don Joseph Ortiz de Otteo, Don Joachin Martínez Guajardo.

This copy agrees with its original, which is filed in the registry in my possession. At the request of the ecclesiastical court, I submit the present copy on one sheet of ordinary, integral paper and one blank sheet, for lack of stamped paper. Witnesses in attendance to its accuracy were Don Francisco Antonio de Rivera y Castro, Don Antonio de Cossío, and Don Juan Ignacio Verridi, residents of this city. Done in this city of Monterrey on February 22, 1758. I, the aforementioned governor and captain general, signed it in front of these witnesses for lack of a public or royal court clerk, to which I attest.

Don Pedro de Barrio Junco y Espriella [signature]
Luis Antonio Gr/a de Pruneda, witness [signature]
Francisco Antonio de Salzedo y Villamill [signature]

Monterrey, [p. 48] February 23, 1758

Remit these original records to the Most Illustrious and Most Reverend Lord Don Fray Francisco de San Buenaventura Martínez de Texada Diez de Velasco, most worthy Bishop of this diocese of Guadajalara of His Majesty's Council so that His Most Illustrious Lordship may decide as he pleases, which will, as always, be for the best. Bachiller Don Francisco Antonio de Larralde, vicario juez eclesiástico of this capital decreed and ordered this before me, to which I attest.

Bachiller Francisco Antonio Larralde [signature]
Before me, José Ignacio Treviño, notary public

Guadalajara, March 29, 1758

Having seen these proceedings, the following are appointed to advise about their resolution: Doctor Don Balthasar Colomo, *canónigo magistral* of this Holy Cathedral Church [holder of the preaching canonry in the cathedral chapter]; Don Pedro Ygnacio Ybarreta, *canónigo doctoral* of said holy church [holder of the academic canonry in the cathedral chapter]; Don Mathías López Prieto, prebend of the same holy church; and the Reverend Father Master Juan Joseph de Villamil of the sacred Company of Jesus. These proceedings are to be given to them, and once they have studied what they contain they are to advise us in the matter, according to their individual specialties. His Most Illustrious Lordship Don Fray Francisco de San Buenaventura [p. 49], Bishop of Guadalajara, of His Majesty's Council will then render the judgment that is advisable. And so he provided, ordered, and signed.

[rubric of the bishop]
Before me, Joseph Sánchez y Lara

In the city of Guadalajara on March 30, 1758.

In accordance with this order, I, the undersigned prosecretary informed Doctor Don Balthasar Colomo, Doctor Don Pedro Ygnacio Ybarreta, Doctor Don Mathías López Prieto, and Reverend Father Master Juan Joseph de Villamil, sacred Company of Jesus, of the preceding decree. Having understood it, they said they would carry it out. So that it may be recorded, I do record it. And I signed it, to which I attest.

Joseph Antonio Sánchez de Lara Torres, prosecretary

Most Illustrious and Most Reverend Father.

In compliance with the preceding decree, the proceedings recorded in these documents have been examined by the persons Your Most Illustrious Lordship [p. 50] chose to entrust with this task. They all agree on the following: there is not sufficient reason to believe that in the events described a miracle occurred, nor to believe that the Most Holy Virgin spoke to the sick woman in question; and they say that they judged it most probable, if not certain, that the vows mentioned in the proceedings are null. They believe that if, perhaps, *coram deo* [in the sight of God] they were valid, the vow of chastity mentioned in them could not be prescribed even by the Roman Pontiff. They are certain that the husband could nullify the vows made by the lady, his wife, and that her confessor could commute the vows for both of them under terms of the Bull[7] or the Most Illustrious Lord Bishop could grant them dispensation if the vows were deemed valid. And, to conclude, any misgivings the aforementioned penitents have, especially in the vow to go to the shrine of Our Lady of Guadalupe, which the husband seems least willing to undertake, might be removed as follows. He has sufficient means that it would not do him considerable harm, and would be a very appropriate thing, that they show in some form their thanks for the truly miraculous benefit received, although it is not that unusual. It would seem best for Your Most Illustrious Lordship to grant dispensation and commutation, substituting in place of what they perhaps had contracted to do with some spiritual exercises such as one of two communions a month for a space of six months or a year, and some alms [p. 51] to which they accede (it being almost certain that the vows are null), in favor of the thing or persons that Your Most Illustrious Lordship may decide would be most pleasing to God, or what seems to you most appropriate, which will be, as always, what is best. Guadalajara, April 7, 1758.

Doctor Balthasar Colomo [signature]
Doctor Pedro Ygnacio Ybarreta [signature]
Doctor Mathías López Prieto [signature]
Juan Joseph de Villamil [signature]

In the city of Guadalajara, April 15, 1758, His Most Illustrious Lordship Don Fray Francisco de San Buenaventura Martines de Texada, Bishop of Guadalajara, New Kingdom of Galicia and León, of the Council of His Majesty (my Lord). Having reviewed these proceedings carried out by order of Bachiller Don Francisco Antonio Larralde, vicario juez eclesiástico of the city of Our Lady of

Monterrey concerning the restored health of Doña María Francisca de Larralde, legitimate wife of Sergeant Major Don Antonio de Urresti, residents of said city, in which it is stated that the aforementioned Doña María Francisca was gravely ill, without hope of recovery and rendered senseless for a span of thirty-six days, at the end of which she returned to her senses and indicated that she wished [p. 52] to receive the Holy Sacrament in the form of the viaticum. Having received it with great devotion and tenderness, she returned to her former near-moribund state, taking very little nourishment because the seriousness of the illness did not allow her to pass food easily. She remained in this state until January 13 of this year, at which time the image of Our Lady, the Most Holy Virgin Mary known as Our Lady of the Walnut Tree, which is venerated in the parish church of the city, was taken to her home. After the image had been there for considerable time, adorned with some pearl bracelets that were gifted to her, and requests being made that, if it was agreeable, she might grant health to the sick woman, the woman recovered consciousness, praising the Blessed Sacrament, Most Holy Mary of Sorrows, and the sweetest name of Jesus, calling by name the parish priest and other priests that they come to see the prodigious event. And she called on her husband, the said Don Antonio de Urresti and, according to some of the witnesses who were deposed, she asked him to join her in chastity for the rest of their lives and to wear next to his skin the habit of Our Father St. Francis and that they go to visit the shrine of Our Lady of Guadalupe in Mexico City, walking the last three and a half leagues. The aforementioned Don Antonio gave his permission for all of this. Her recovery continued up to February 7 when she returned to her former state of grave illness, remaining in that state until the seventeenth of the same month when they carried her on her bed to the church and placed her before Our Lady. There she came to and, with gestures, asked to be taken to [p. 53] kiss the image, which she did, asking also by signs to be taken to the convent of St. Francis where she prayed to the Blessed Sacrament and the sovereign image of the Nazarene. By signs, she indicated that God Our Lord was calling her and her husband to the religious life, and indicated also that she would not speak until she was in the presence of the Most Illustrious Lord Bishop.

Having seen also the writing presented on behalf of the aforementioned Don Antonio de Urresti and Doña María Francisca de Larralde in which they express that said Doña María Francisca was moved by the fear of death, or not being altogether in her right mind when she made the vows that have been communicated to your Most Illustrious

Lordship, and concluding that for the well-being of their consciences his Most Illustrious Lordship might declare the vows null, or if they are valid in whole or in part, to commute them or grant dispensation. They further offer to attend promptly to whatever penitence is imposed in their place, and the rest that they have communicated privately to his Most Illustrious Lordship.

Considering also the opinion of doctors Don Balthasar Colomo, canónigo magistral, Don Pedro Ygnacio Ybarreta, canónigo doctoral, Don Mathías Prieto, prebend of this holy cathedral church, and the Reverend Father Master Juan Joseph de Villamil, professor of theology in the College of the Sacred Company of Jesus of this city, in which they suggest that the proceedings do not provide a basis to believe that a miracle caused the sick woman's recovery. Furthermore, they judge [p. 54] that most probably, but not certainly, the aforementioned vows are null, and that even in case they are valid in the sight of God, not even the supreme pontiff is empowered to impose the vow of chastity under the circumstances in which he was made and the rest of what the proceedings establish, in which your Lordship concurred.

Therefore, His Most Illustrious Lordship declared that the aforementioned Don Antonio de Urresti and Doña María Francisca de Larralde are under no obligation to fulfill the said vows. Moreover, and for the greater well-being of their consciences, His Most Illustrious Lordship, using the authority granted to him under civil law and for the special benefit of the Holy Apostolic See, granted a dispensation for the said vows. In consideration of the reasonable considerations they have privately communicated to His Most Illustrious Lordship and the consent of the said Don Antonio de Urresti and Doña María Francisca de Larralde, he commuted the visit to Our Lady of Guadalupe to 500 pesos, applied to the building fund of the parish church of the city of Monterrey, and on the day they choose they shall cause a sung mass to be celebrated to the aforementioned Most Holy Lady at the altar or chapel that may exist in the same parish church, and they shall stay there to keep vigil for the rest of the day, and wear the habit of St. Francis for two years or the period her husband, Don Antonio Urresti, may otherwise agree to, wearing it over ordinary, modest clothing whenever he/she/they go to church.[8] And he ordered that they be given an exact version of this decree for safekeeping. Thus his Most Illustrious Lordship ordered and signed.

Fray Francisco de San Buenaventura, Bishop of Guadalajara [signature]
Before me, Doctor Don Matheo Joseph de Arteaga, secretary

PART II

Our Lady in the Kernel of Corn

*M*arian apparitions and miraculous images in Mexico inevitably bring to mind one renowned figure—Our Lady of Guadalupe and its shrine at Tepeyac in the Valley of Mexico. Guadalupe is, indeed, a touchstone to the history of Catholicism and popular devotion in Mexico, and Mexico is a special case of a religious image becoming the main symbol for an emerging nation. As Jeannette Rodríguez recently wrote, "To be of Mexican descent is to recognize the image of Our Lady of Guadalupe." But devotion to Our Lady of Guadalupe has a history. This image has not always been, and in some ways still is not, the dominant symbol throughout Mexico, and the location of its principal shrine on the edge of Mexico City is as much a key to its importance as is its association with the oldest Marian apparition officially recognized by the Catholic Church. Dozens of different shrines to other miraculous images have captured the hearts of thousands, sometimes millions of followers in Mexico. They still do.

One of the puzzles about this most famous of Mexican images of Mary is how little is known about the devotion during its first century or so. Until 1648, we have no written account of the story of the apparitions of Mary to Juan Diego in 1531 and the image of Mary revealed on his cloak when he opened it to spread roses from Tepeyac before Bishop Zumárraga. Written accounts of apparition stories for miraculous images in Europe and America often were set down many years after the events they describe, so the case of Guadalupe is not unusual in this respect. But, in all such cases, it becomes uncertain whether the apparition stories were products of untold revisions and refinements in a long oral tradition or were mainly the formulations of those who wrote them down much later.

The following set of records of the ecclesiastical court of the Archdiocese of Mexico, now filed in the Archivo General de la Nación

(*Bienes Nacionales* 1086 expediente 10), provides several accounts of the discovery of a miraculous image of Mary that were recorded much closer in time to the events described. Those events occurred in 1774 in Tlamacazapa, an Indian village in the parish of Acamixtla, not far from the silver mines of Taxco in the highlands of central Mexico. The records consist of two accounts of the discovery of the image written by the parish priest of Acamixtla, Bernardino de Mesa, plus depositions before the ecclesiastical judge of the Archdiocese of Mexico (the provisor and vicar general) by this priest, Anna María (the Indian woman who discovered the image), her husband, and one of their sons. They offer a glimpse of an incipient devotion and the somewhat different stories told about it at the beginning.

In this case, the devotion seems to have had no more than a beginning. The image of Mary—contained in a kernel of corn—was presented to the ecclesiastical judge at the time of the depositions, and there is no evidence that it was returned to the parish priest or Anna María. No further documentation about the image appears in this file or other records that survive from the colonial archive of the Archdiocese of Mexico. The documentation dates from 1774, but a cover sheet was added in 1783, as if the records and the kernel of corn were then placed in an inactive file.

These records provide an opportunity to glimpse an apparition story taking shape in the late eighteenth century, one that was not altogether acceptable to higher church authorities. Even if the basic story sprang from local circumstances and expectations, those expectations drew upon long experience of recounting miracle stories, with their strong tendency to follow known patterns, if not stereotypes. A miracle story may exemplify a style demanded by the evolving process of formal recognition by the Church. At the same time, it may draw upon other, usually older, expectations for a proper story. In comparison to most Spanish and Spanish American miracle stories from the sixteenth to eighteenth centuries, this one is unusual in centering on a pious woman in her home, rather than a boy or man in some desolate location far from home. But it fits with growing interest in Spain and America in the advocation of Our Lady of Sorrows (Nuestra Señora de los Dolores) during the seventeenth and eighteenth centuries, especially by pregnant women. The priest gets carried away with this association in his first account, but it is present in Anna María's deposition, and perhaps expresses the participating neighbors' account to the priest, as he claimed. Were he and the other men in this record appropriating a budding female devotion that centered on childbirth and childbirth suffering?

The records of Our Lady in a kernel of corn also provide intriguing, if incidental, evidence of devotion in a colonial Indian household—among

other things, a home altar, the different occupations and spiritual preoccupations of this husband and wife, and the distant and muffled dialogue
with priests (who visited the village for a hurried mass on Sundays and
the Easter Duty) and the schoolmaster who was responsible for teaching
the rudiments of Catholic doctrine but spoke only Spanish. The diminu-
tive image of the loving mother of God discovered at home reminds
me of the ceramic figurines so often recovered by archaeologists from
the debris of house sites in precolonial central Mexico, perhaps there
to protect family members and insure a good harvest. The discovery
of Our Lady in the kernel of corn was a domestic moment, but it was
also understood by authorities in Mexico City to be subversive—the
tiny image of Our Lady mixed among the seed corn waiting to be recognized and adopted in this transient form by a worthy (female, untu-
tored, devout, Indian) eye. The authorities were quick to acquire it and
then make it disappear.

More than a few mysteries remain in the several accounts in these
records. (1) The discrepancies between the priest's two accounts of the
apparition are puzzling, and his surprising explanation may or may not
be designed to hide gullible elaboration on his part. And his explanation
of the discrepancies raises questions about a vanishing baby, who only
eats twice a day! (2) Neither of the priest's accounts is quite the same
as Anna María's testimony. (3) The ecclesiastical court took no interest
in the subsequent marvels associated with this image of Mary that the
priest described in his first account. We want to know more. (4) And
as a case record, the file is incomplete. Not only is the parish priest's
initial "opinion" missing, there is no opinion offered in writing by the
ecclesiastical judge and no notation about any subsequent review. The
ecclesiastical court seems to have suspended the inquiry after the depositions were taken on November 23 and 24, 1774. The court apparently
retained the image, thereby suppressing an incipient devotion that had
been endorsed wholeheartedly by the parish priest in his first written
account. If this is, in fact, what happened, why did the ecclesiastical
judge decide on this course of action (or, better said, inaction)?

Document

First version [by Bernardo de Mesa]

Acount of the prodigious miracle by Most Holy Mary in the village of Santa María de la Asumpción Tlamacazapa, parish of Acamixtla, appearing as the figure of Divine Grace (Alta Gracia[1]) in a kernel of corn to an Indian woman about to give birth (1774)

Anna María, Indian of the village of Tlamacazapa, married to Miguel Juan reports that on March 25 of this year, 1774, the day of the Incarnate Word and the Sorrows of Most Holy Mary, at about nine in the morning, her husband said to her as he was about to leave: "My daughter, it may rain tonight. If it does, tomorrow I want to sow my cornfield (if it is God's will). In the meantime, I am going to help my compadre build his fence. You can sort out for seed the best grain in that jar of corn, and put the bad ones aside." Having said this, he left. At about eleven thirty, she began to sort out the best kernels in the jar. Holding in her hand five kernels from the ears of corn she had been shucking, she fell asleep. This drowsiness was great and sudden, for when she began to shuck the ears of corn she had been wide awake. But sleep overcame her at that moment and she had to lie down. Being very close to giving birth, in her sleep she felt some mild pains. They awakened her and she said, "Most Holy Virgin, please help me, for I am about to give birth, with no one to help me." At that moment she was alone with her eight-year-old son, Francisco Pasqual. And saying this, she opened her hand which held the kernels of corn. She looked at them and saw that the one on top contained an image that appeared to be that of the Virgin. At that same instant she called her son to see if what she thought must be a dream was true. The little boy rejoiced, "Mother, it is the Virgin, it's the Virgin." Seeing her son's reaction, she cast aside the other kernels and handed this one to him, telling him to wrap it in paper and place it in the chest until his father returned. "He will tell us whether or not it is the image of the Virgin."

At that moment, without a midwife or other assistance than her invocation of Most Holy Mary and the helpless company of her young son, she gave birth, with gentle pains, unlike any she had experienced before (her previous birthings had all been rough and dangerous, and this one was almost painless). After the birth she sent her son to find the midwife and her sister-in-law, who found her safe and sound, as if she had not just given birth. They did no more than clean and wrap the infant. Anna María told them of the wonder that had taken place, which she repeated to her husband when he returned at evening prayers (*a la oración*—vespers). Their son ran out to the street to tell him that the Virgin had appeared to his mother. In disbelief, the father entered the house without realizing that his wife had given birth. She shouted to him that it was true, that an image of the Virgin had appeared and that he should look in the chest and see for himself. He did so, and seeing that it was true, he put it back for safekeeping and approached his wife and asked why she was lying down. She replied, "I have given birth without the aid of a midwife, thanks to Most Holy Mary." Astonished by this marvel, he kept it secret, fearing the pastor who was always preaching to them about the abomination of idolatry. Also, he still doubted whether it was right or not to express devotion to that image since he did not know from a knowledgeable person if it was the Virgin's doing. Because of this fear he did not show the image to anyone for six or eight days. Then he showed it to his brother, Francisco Gaspar, who advised him not to express devotion to the image until it had been shown to the schoolmaster of the village. Although his brother urged him to take the image to the schoolmaster that very hour, he kept it until the day of Christ's Ascension [forty days after Easter]. That day, after the priest had said mass and left town, he gave it to the schoolmaster, who kept it in his possession until the next Sunday when he gave it to the pastor, who gave it to the parish priest.

From a very young age, this Indian woman has been very pious, very devoted to Most Holy Mary in her fasts and prayers. The infant is so content that she makes no fuss even to be fed, taking the breast no more than once in twelve hours. She was baptized Juana Ramos since the baptism took place on Palm Sunday and this is the custom among them.

The circumstances described here make this a more wondrous case even than the sacred apparition of Our Lady of Guadalupe because cloth is less perishable than a kernel of corn, especially in these parts, where harvested corn does not last even a full year, and the kernel in which the image appeared is from last year and is so solid and intact that it looks like a crystal. The body of the image takes up most of the kernel of corn; the rays consist of the outer skin, which has become transparent. The image and the rays appear perfect from any angle.

It has come to the parish priest's notice (and he is prepared to swear to it *in verbo sacerdotis*) that the image has become more perfect by the day, for now one sees a triangle above the most holy head, symbol of the August Trinity. And it has an outline around the image that is so subtle only the Almighty could have formed it.

The events in question took place at three in the afternoon.

[Also noteworthy] is the abundance of corn throughout the land this year. It is a glory, and causes rejoicing, to see the abundant crops and all the rest that has happened. About all of this the fortunate Indian woman is prepared to testify.

Second version [by Bernardo de Mesa]

Account of the apparition of Most Holy Mary in a kernel of corn in the village of Tlamacazapan, parish of Acamixtla, to Anna María, Indian married to Miguel Juan, on Friday, May 6 of the present year, 1774, as follows.

Anna María, Indian married to Miguel Juan, of the village of Tlamacapazan, parish of Acamixtla, says: On a rainy Thursday morning, May 5 of this year, her husband told her that if it rained again on Friday, he was going to sow his field of corn and that she should sort out the seed to plant. Following her husband's instructions, after he left that morning to help a compadre build a fence, after sunrise she set about sorting the seed corn. She took it from a jar of kernels that had already been removed from the cobs. She set aside only three measures of grain that had not spoiled and put them on the table that served as an altar, saying to Our Lady of Sorrows and Saint Isidore the Farmer, "Mother and Lady of mine, saintly Saint Isidore, please pardon me for not lighting candles because I am a poor woman and have no money to buy them. But I offer you this incense (which she, in fact, placed on the table of the little household altar) so that you may bless this seed and protect it from locusts and other harm since you see how poor we are." Having made this fervent entreaty, her husband returned at evening prayers and she told him that she had only found three measures of grain and if it rained that night he could begin to plant them and she would shuck more corn the next day.

That Thursday night it did not rain as expected, and Anna María's husband decided not to begin planting on Friday. Instead, he left to

continue helping his compadre with the fence. After midday, having
finished grinding corn for tortillas and eating, she began to sort the
seed corn that was left in the jar from the day before. She spread the
grain out on a *petate* or new straw mat, bringing it in a basket from
the jar to the petate. In spreading it out with her hand, one kernel
rested on the top. Her attention was drawn to it and she realized that
it contained an image of the Virgin. Closing her hand around it, she
continued sorting the grain until she called to her seven-and-a-half-
year-old son, Francisco, who was with another, younger son of hers.
She showed him the grain of corn and said, "Look, son, this kernel
of corn seems to be the Virgin of Sorrows." The boy tried to take the
kernel from her hand, which she did not allow, saying with a joyous
expression on his face, "Mother, it is her," which his little brother,
Domingo de la Cruz, repeated. Anna María's sister-in-law, Francisca
Antonia, who lives next door, heard the boys and ran to their house
asking what had been found. Anna María replied that that image had
been found among the seed corn. Then two other women came in, one
her sister-in-law, Teresa María, and her husband's sister-in-law named
María Juana. All were astonished, and told her that it was an image of
Our Lady and that she should protect it in a piece of paper with great
reverence in order to show to her husband when he returned.

Her husband returned at evening prayers, and before he came
into the house his son Francisco told him that his mommy [*nana*] had
found an image of the Virgin in a kernel of corn. The boy's father did
not believe it until his wife showed the kernel to him. Astonished, he
expressed his adoration, saying that it was an image of the Virgin, and
he wrapped it in paper and placed it in a box for safekeeping.

The next day, Saturday, his brother Francisco Gaspar came to visit
him at nightfall. Miguel Juan showed him the kernel of corn and he, too,
marveled at it and said it was the image of Most Holy Mary. Putting it
back for safekeeping, they decided that the following day before mass
they would show the image to the schoolmaster of the village so that he
could show it to the pastor. Francisco Gaspar did this because he knows
how to speak Spanish and the schoolmaster does not speak Nahuatl.
Having seen the image, the schoolmaster asked how they had found
it, and he kept it to show the priest. He forgot to show it to the priest
that Sunday, but did so the following Sunday, May 15, the day of Saint
Isidore the Farmer. In the interim, Anna María pressed her husband to
bring the image back to her, worried that it might be lost. But she did
not succeed because the schoolmaster had given it to the pastor, who
had given it to the parish priest. She is prepared to testify to all of this,
if necessary, and her parish priest and curate will provide information

about her personal conduct, that she has always been a devotee of Most Holy Mary under the advocation of the Sorrows, and from a young age has fasted in her honor.

Marvelous portents of Mary's generosity have been evident recently. Since the image was brought to the parish priest's residence two weeks ago (which is where it is displayed, with as much decency as possible, until your Most Illustrious Prelacy may make other provision), every woman in labor who has invoked it has given birth successfully; a child one year old who was brought in nearly dead was lifted by its mother in front of the image, in the presence of the parish priest and the family, and is now well and sound. All the people from surrounding places, and even from farther away, are visiting Our Lady and anxiously desire that the image be placed so that all can see it and venerate it. Your Most Illustrious Highness will, in your benevolence, decide where it should be placed and the indulgences and privileges that may be deemed appropriate.

[DEPOSITIONS]

In the City of Mexico, quarters of Dr. Joseph Ruiz de Conejares, Governor, Provisor, and Vicar General of this archdiocese, on November 23, 1774, Br. Bernardino de Mesa appeared. As parish priest and ecclesiastical judge in the district of Acamixtla of this archdiocese, it is he who composed and sent to the Most Illustrious Archbishop of this archdiocese the accounts of the apparition of Our Lady, prepared according to form, that precede the record of these [today's] proceedings. He offered to speak the truth about what he may know and be asked, which was in the following manner:

First, he was ordered to examine the aforementioned opinion, dated in the parish of Acamixtla on September 20 of the present year, as well as the account which accompanied it of the miraculous apparition of Our Most Holy Lady Mary in a kernel of corn, which is identified at the beginning with the words *First Version*, in the margin, and also another account of the same apparition identified in the margin with the words *Second Version*.

Asked if the said written opinion and first account are the ones he directed to His Most Illustrious Highness [the archbishop] and if the second account is the one he presented yesterday to the present Provisor and Vicar General, he replied that the written opinion and first account are the very ones he sent to His Most Illustrious Highness on the aforementioned date, and that the second account is also the one that he presented yesterday to the Provisor and Vicar General of this archdiocese.

He was presented with the image of Our Lady that is said to have appeared miraculously in the kernel of corn and is housed in a little monstrance about eight inches high, and in the center of its rays the image is displayed between two pieces of glass, in a little gold circle. Upon inspection he said it was the same one that he gave to the Provisor and Vicar General yesterday, the one said to have appeared to Anna María, Indian of the village of Tlamacazapa in the district of the aforementioned parish.

Asked to describe the circumstances of this apparition according to the faithful account he has made of it and information he may have gathered, he said that according to the most exact information he has gathered from the Indian Anna María, her husband Miguel Juan, and a son just over seven and a half years old named Francisco, the circumstances surrounding the apparition of the said image are those referred to in the second account.

Asked how it was that the second account of the circumstances of the apparition of Our Lady—deemed certain according to the Indian Anna María, her husband Miguel Joan, and their son, Francisco—is so different from the account he rendered in the first version, he replied that the differences result from the fact that the first version was composed from testimony of the Indians who gathered at Anna María's house, and the second version was provided by Anna María, her husband, and their son, which is more reliable, since they were the ones immediately touched by the marvel, if such it was, and not the others.

Asked about the habits and circumstances of the Indian Anna María, her conduct, Christian behavior, virtues, and anything else, he said that she has been exemplary, always dedicating herself to virtuous works such as attending church often, offering her prayers there, and demonstrating her affection and devotion to Our Lady. In his six years as head of the said parish, nothing has been alleged against her that is worthy of note. She is quite unique and of proven virtue among the Indians.

Asked if he considered the aformentioned Indian, Anna María, and her husband Miguel Juan sufficiently skilled, trained, and industrious to have made the image that appears in the kernel of corn, and in this way to have confected it and spread the word about the apparition, he said that the husband and wife have all the guilelessness that is natural among the Indians, and for that reason he not only is persuaded that they do not have the ability and industriousness to have created the image in the kernel of corn in the form that it can be observed now, but that he also believes them incapable of having feigned and promoted its appearance as miraculous.

Asked if in the aforementioned village of Tlamacazapa or in some other community in the district of his parish or others nearby he knows of some individual who has the ability and industriousness to have created the said image, or if the Indian husband and wife have been in contact with someone capable of creating it and promoting it as miraculous, he said that neither in the communities of his parish nor in those nearby does he know of anyone capable of creating the image in this form, nor does he know of any person known to the couple who would be capable of creating it.

Asked if in light of what he has declared in his second account and observed since the image was placed in his care he considered it to be a truly miraculous apparition, he said that he considers it miraculous in the sense that such a perfect figure of Our Lady represented in a tiny kernel of corn could not be natural; and that no one has ever seen a kernel of corn like it.

At this point His Lordship concluded this testimony for the time being, reserving the possibility of continuing it if the results and circumstances of these proceedings warrant. And the witness was instructed, under pain of excommunication, to hold this matter in complete secrecy until the Most Illustrious Archbishop or the present Provisor decides otherwise. Having read this his declaration, he swore that he affirmed and ratified it, and he signed, along with the said Provisor whom I recognize as such. The witness is the head priest of said parish.

[signed by Dr. Joseph Ruiz de Conejares and Bernardino de Mesa, in the presence of the senior notary, Joachin de Lasturayn]

In the aforementioned place, day, month, and year, Anna María, Indian of the village of Tlamacazapa, married to Miguel Juan of the parish of Acamixtla, appeared. She seems to be twenty-four or twenty-five years old. Through the interpreter Bachiller Joseph Julián Ramírez, priest and professor of the Nahuatl language in the Royal University of this city, the Provisor and Vicar General of this archdiocese received her sworn promise to tell the truth about what she might know and be asked. And being asked for her name, status, residence, and age, she said her name is Anna María, Indian resident of the aforementioned Tlamacazapa, parish of San Martín Acamixtla, married to Miguel Juan. She does not know her age (which is common among Indians), but seems to be the age already noted, judging by her appearance.

Asked if she has some particular and special devotion to Most Holy Mary, she said that she does. She commends herself daily to Mary's care and devotes herself to sweeping her village's church, burning incense, lighting candles, and praying to her. In all of her necessities she commends herself particularly to this Lady under the title and advocation of the Sorrows.

Asked if she has received some special favor from Most Holy Mary on the occasions that she has invoked her, she said that generally she experiences and has experienced Most Holy Mary's protection on the occasions in which he has invoked her and sought her protection.

Asked if at some time Our Lady has appeared to her, she said that one Friday afternoon, when she was sorting corn and separating the good kernels from those that were spoiled so that her husband could plant his field, she discovered an image of Our Lady of Sorrows in one of the kernels of corn. Acting on this surprising event, she took hold of this kernel and held it in her hand. Her son, Francisco Gaspar, about eight years old, asked her what she had in her hand. When she showed it to him, he said it was the Virgin of Sorrows.

Asked if she would recognize the Virgin that appeared in the corn if she saw it, she said yes. When it was brought to her and taken from the little monstrance, she said it was the one she had found in the kernel of corn.

Asked to whom she had shown it that day and in the following days, she said that she showed it to three sisters-in-law named Francisca Antonia, Teresa María, and María Joana, and to her husband the night of that Friday when he returned from working on a fence with a compadre of his. Her husband had first news of it from their son who went out to tell him before he reached the house that his mother had an image of the Virgin.

Asked where she kept it, she said it was wrapped in paper in a box until the following Sunday morning when she gave it to a brother-in-law named Francisco Gaspar who knows the Spanish language so that he would show it to the schoolmaster. From that day to this day she had not seen it again because that same Sunday her brother-in-law gave it to the priest who said mass in the village. She does not know the priest's name. He was neither the parish priest nor an assistant in the parish.

Asked what month and day the apparition occurred, and on what date she gave it up, she said her husband told her it was in May, but she does not know the day except that it was a Friday that she found the image and the following Sunday that it was given to the priest.

Asked if there is a day of the week in which she makes a special voluntary sacrifice in honor of Our Lady, she said that except when she is nursing, she fasts on Fridays in devotion to the Sorrows of Most Holy Mary, especially when she is pregnant, to implore her help in giving birth.

Asked if this year or in previous years she has fulfilled the Easter Duty to confess and take communion, and if she is accustomed to confessing and taking communion sometimes during the year, she said that in all the preceding years she has fulfilled the Easter Duty and this year she confessed during Lent when she was sick. During the year she does not confess because there is no opportunity to do so since on Sundays and holidays only one priest comes to their villages to say mass.

Here, it being late, the testimony was concluded for the time being, reserving the possibility of continuing it whenever it might be deemed appropriate. The record was read to the interpreter who said that to the best of his understanding it was what the aforementioned Anna María had said. She did not sign because she does not know how. The interpreter signs with Your Lordship, to which I witness, Thursday, November.

[signed by Dr. Joseph Ruiz de Conejares and Joseph Ramírez, in the presence of Joachin de Lasturayn, chief notary]

In Mexico City, in the quarters of the Governador and Vicar General on November 24, 1774, Miguel Juan, Indian of the village of Tlamacazapa, married to Anna María, appeared. Through Br. Joseph Ramírez, priest and professor of the Nahuatl language in the Royal and Pontifical University of this city and synodal examiner of the language in this archdiocese, Your Lordship received his testimony. Under oath he promised to tell the truth about what he might know and be asked. Asked for his name, status, residence, and age, he said he is Miguel Juan, Indian, native of the village of Tlamacazapa, parish of San Martín Acamixtla, married to Anna María. He does not know his age although, based on his appearance, he is about twenty-five years old.

Asked if he lives in peace with his wife, if in the time they have been married she has been the cause of vexation, and if she has lived in a Christian way and according to her station as a married woman, he said that he has noted no vice or peccadillo of any kind. On the contrary, she has always behaved very well, and that in the ten years of their marriage there have not been quarrels or upsets of any kind; rather, they have lived together in the appropriate peace and harmony.

Asked if he knows whether his wife, Anna María, has some particular and special devotion to some saint, how does she give evidence of it, and what else does he know about it, he said that he knows that his wife, Anna María, is particularly devoted to Most Holy Mary of Sorrows, and he knows it because she invokes her often, and in times of need she implores her for her aid and protection.

Asked if he knows whether Our Lady of the Sorrows has done some special favor for his wife, he said that he does not know.

Asked if his wife has found some image of Our Lady of Sorrows, how she found it, and what kind of image it was, he said that he knows his wife found an image of Our Lady of Sorrows in the kernel of corn, that she found it among many others when she was sorting the seed corn. This occurred on a Friday in the month of May at three in the afternoon. He knew of this because when he returned home after working on a fence, his eight-year-old son, Francisco Gaspar, told him, and he confirmed it when he saw the image, which his wife showed him.

Asked if he put the aforementioned image in among those kernels of corn or has knowledge that someone else did so, he said that he did not put it there, nor does he know that anyone else may have done so.

Asked if he would recognize the image if it were brought before him, he said yes. And when it was presented to him, he said it was the same one that his wife showed him on the aforementioned day.

Asked if he asked his wife how she discovered the image, and what she said to him, he said that, yes, he had asked her, and the account she gave him was that while sorting the shucked maize for planting that afternoon, she had found it among the kernels. It was the one in which the image of Our Lady appeared. Having separated it from the others, she kept it in her hand and showed it to their son. When he returned from work his son told him that the Virgin had appeared to his mother. For this reason he asked his wife about the apparition and she told him what he has declared here.

Asked where they kept the image, what they did thereafter, and to whom they gave it, he said they kept it in a box wrapped in paper until the next Sunday when, as the bell was calling the community to mass, he gave it to his brother, Francisco Gaspar, who knows how to speak the Spanish language, who showed it and gave it to the schoolmaster to show and give it to the priest who said mass that day. And, in fact, it was given to the said priest who was astonished to see it. Having to go on to say mass in another village, the priest placed it for safekeeping in a pocket of his cassock and took it with him.

Asked for the name and surname of the aforementioned priest and where he resides, and whether he is one of the curates or lieutenants of the parish, he said that the priest is named Don Joseph, but he does not know his surname or place of residence. He is not a curate or lieutenant of the parish priest because the parish priest makes indiscriminate use of both secular and regular priests to say mass in the village.

Asked if he has seen the aforementioned image since the day they gave it to the schoolmaster and the priest, he said that he has not seen it since then.

Asked if he knows to whom the said priest gave the image thereafter, he said he did not know.

Asked if he has completed the Easter Duty to confess and take communion this year and in the past, he said that has fulfilled this duty every year.

At this point, the testimony was concluded with the possibility that it could be continued whenever it was deemed necessary. The record was read to the interpreter, who said it was, as best he understood it, what the Indian Miguel Juan had declared. Miguel Juan did not sign because he said he did not know how, and Your Lordship did so with the aforementioned interpreter, to which I bear witness.

[signed by Dr. Joseph Ruiz de Conejares and Joseph Ramírez, in the presence of Joachin de Lasturayn, senior notary]

In the aforementioned place, day, month, and year, an Indian boy who said his name is Francisco Gaspar, appeared. He is the son of Miguel Juan and Anna María, Indians of the village of Tlamacazapa. He seems to be about seven or eight years old. Through the interpreter he was asked some very elementary questions about Christian doctrine. He proved completely ignorant of them because, as it was explained, even though he attends school, he cannot understand the Spanish language in which the schoolmaster explains and teaches the doctrine. When asked about the circumstances surrounding the discovery of the image of Our Lady in the kernel of corn, to which his mother refers in her declaration, and of which he told his father, he answered consistently in every particular. And also, when the kernel of corn in which the image of the Virgin appears was taken from the little monstrance and shown to him, he said it was the same one that his mother had closed in her hand and showed him the day she discovered it.

This is what resulted from the questions put to him through the interpreter, who signed it with the Provisor, to which I bear witness.

[signed by Dr. Joseph Ruiz de Conejares and Joseph Ramírez, in the presence of Joachin de Lasturayn, senior notary]

PART III

Between Nativitas and Mexico City

Miracles and the Mundane in an Eighteenth-Century Pastor's Local Religion

*P*arish priests were more than spokesmen for official doctrine and institutional order; more than orchestrators of a universal liturgy; more than gatekeepers of the sacred in the face of exuberant or tepid popular faith. They carried their own accumulated religious experience, enthusiasms, and networks of affiliation, friendship, and knowledge with them into pastoral service. A seminary education, ordination, liturgical duties, and career ladder did not wash away all the personal habits of faith they brought to the priesthood. The devotional practices they knew from childhood; their preference for particular saints and representations of Mary, holidays, scriptural passages, prayers, places, and miracle stories; their talents and inclinations as public figures and practitioners of the faith; and their foibles and sense of calling to the priesthood all came into play. This side of pastors at work is not often documented in more than fleeting glimpses, but here is an exception—a more sustained account in one pastor's words. It is largely the story of Francisco Antonio de la Rosa Figueroa, an eighteenth-century Franciscan friar of the Province of the Holy Gospel headquartered in Mexico City. The place and time are his period of service as pastor of the *doctrina* (proto-parish) of Nativitas Tepetlatcingo, an Indian *pueblo* about eight miles south of downtown Mexico City, during 1739–1740 and 1743–1745. Father de la Rosa's account of his time in Nativitas and miracles worked through an image of the Virgin Mary he found there determines this focus. Composed in 1775 and 1776, near the end of his life, its tight lines fill both sides of twenty-two folio sheets. His labors, passions, quirky personality, and checkered career fairly spring from these pages of his shaky script as he relived his transcendent moment and acted on a desire to keep alive the devotion to this special image of Mary.

There is more to Father de la Rosa's account than I have presented in this essay,[1] which I hope invites the reader into his story of Our Lady of the Intercession in other ways. I mainly address two features of the text that bear on his faith and activities as pastor. One is the bifocal vision of place and time in his presentation of miracles: Nativitas and Mexico City; and the 1740s events and the 1775–1776 composition of the text. The other is his view of Nativitas's Indian parishioners—mainly as impediments or, at best, incidental witnesses more than protagonists in the story he tells of divine presence at work in the world. Father de la Rosa's personality, opinions, and enthusiasms come through strongly in his text, but his parishioners are heard in it, too. I have given the parishioners a larger and different place in the story of local history and practices than he does by considering his treatment of them in light of other documentation about the community in the eighteenth century and other ways of reckoning with their activities. In discussing de la Rosa himself I have also reached beyond his own narrative to the record of his career that he would not have thought essential to the story at hand or how he remembered his life.

The Pastor and His Text

Francisco de la Rosa's background and career take shape in scattered administrative records and glancing remarks in his text. Mexico City was the pivotal point of his life, even during his residence elsewhere in central Mexico. He was born there in 1698, the only child of Creole Spanish parents. His father and several other members of the extended family were traders and shopkeepers. His father eventually served as *alcalde mayor* (district governor) in two marginal districts, but was removed for misappropriation of funds and died in penury, in the care of his son. De la Rosa began his religious vocation comparatively late, and with two false starts, first as a Dominican novice in Mexico City in 1722 or 1723. He requested release from his vows soon thereafter, became a Franciscan novice in the Convento Recoleto de San Cosmé in August 1723, again asked to leave after four months, and spent the following year in Chalcatzingo (Morelos) studying Nahuatl with the parish priest. He was readmitted to the Franciscan novitiate in May 1725 with the understanding that his earlier false starts had been "without blemish of any kind," and was ordained in the Province of the Holy Gospel and approved for pastoral duty by 1733.[2] At some point in the 1730s he was also licensed to do notarial work for the Inquisition. He was particularly proud of this association, and continued to correspond with Inquisition judges on matters of faith long after he left pastoral service.

De la Rosa opened his account of Nativitas's miraculous image of Mary with his own history of unhappy pastoral assignments, first in 1734 as assistant pastor in Tepepan, an Indian community in the Valley of Mexico near Xochimilco with a small shrine to Our Lady of los Remedios. After unspecified troubles with parishioners there,[3] he was in Cuernavaca the next year when a group of zealous Spanish Franciscans from the newly established Colegio de San Fernando in Mexico City arrived to preach and hear confessions. "This mission so startled my spirit and so moved my inclination to the missionary's life that I immediately decided to seek a way to leave the ministry among Indians and enter the College of San Fernando," he wrote. Anxious to become part of their exalted enterprise of spiritual revival and leave behind the aggravations and tedium of a ministry among Indians, he applied for membership. But after a month's residence at the college he was denied a permanent place among the missionary preachers—denied, he thought, because just one member opposed him—and returned to the home monastery of his province in Mexico City.

After brief and unhappy appointments in several other Indian communities of central Mexico,[4] he was assigned in 1739 to Nativitas Tepetlatcingo, south of Mexico City on the road to Coyoacán. There he found a small, rundown establishment, and few signs of spiritual life. "The little cloister," he wrote melodramatically, "seemed suspended in air; the church and sacristy crumbling; the walls riddled with harmful salt deposits; the paraphernalia of the liturgy absolutely indecent because of the Indians' filthiness; the store of possessions did not correspond to the written inventory; the account book was as full of crossouts and erasures as the inventory. Considering all this, my blood froze."

On the advice of his friend Antonio Ramírez del Castillo, Vicar General of the Archdiocese of Mexico, Father de la Rosa had Nativitas's rough wooden statue of the Virgin Mary reshaped by an Indian sculptor in Tlatelolco. (Tlatelolco was one of the two major Indian districts of Mexico City. The other, San Juan, has an even more important place in this story that de la Rosa passes over.) To his astonishment the statue was transformed into an object of exquisite beauty. He moved quickly to have it richly attired with gold jewelry, pearls, and its own splendid wig and eyelashes. A "sacred magnet of hearts," he called it at one point, "celestial pearl" at another. He and the vicar general hit upon the idea of displaying the image in Mexico City in order to increase its fame, raise funds for rebuilding the convent and church at Nativitas, and cover other costs of serving Our Lady. According to de la Rosa's account, the spirituality of the Indian parishioners was rekindled by their beautified statue, and they encouraged him in his plans to dignify the devotion with building projects and promote it beyond the pueblo. He noted in passing that elders from the pueblo always guarded the statue on its visits to the city.

Father de la Rosa started to promote the devotion to this image of Our Lady and rebuild the church and convent, but within a year he was transferred, first to Xochitepec, Morelos, and then to Santa María la Redonda, an Indian doctrina in Mexico City. Reluctantly he complied. (Indeed, these transfers may have been intended to teach an overactive spirit a lesson in obedience. He was quick to assure his Franciscan readers in 1775 that he always obeyed superior orders, as if there might be some lingering doubt.) Dispirited by the indifference and disobedience of his parishioners in Santa María la Redonda and broken in health, he tried to resign after less than two years there.[5]

To his surprise and delight, he was reassigned to Nativitas in 1743. Warming to the challenge, he set to work collecting money, materials, expert advice, and labor to rebuild the church and convent. He added a secure little roadside chapel for prayers and donations by passersby, furnishing it with a fine painting of his beloved statue of Our Lady, which he called Nuestra Señora del Patrocinio (Our Lady of Intercession). As his trips with the statue to the homes of wealthy residents of the capital became more frequent, the fame of the statue in the city seems to have grown. His ambitious plans and popular devotion in the city culminated in a great rosary procession of the statue through the center of the city during the Feast of the Immaculate Conception in early December 1743. According to de la Rosa's account, it was a lavish and joyful, yet decorous affair, with crowds of people following the statue into the cathedral and on to a special service he conducted at the Church of Regina Coeli (Queen of Heaven). Now, with popular devotion at a glorious peak and a succession of miracles about to begin, Father de la Rosa was leading the spiritual revival he had dreamed of among the Fernandine friars in 1735.

But the story of public devotion to Nuestra Señora del Patrocinio soon took an abrupt turn, largely unexplained in de la Rosa's telling. By the fall of 1744 his superiors denied him permission to take the statue to Mexico City,[6] and before another year passed he was removed from Nativitas and assigned to the archive and library of his home monastery in Mexico City, remaining there until his death in 1777. The excitement about Nativitas's image of Nuestra Señora del Patrocinio, at least in Mexico City, seems to have cooled about as fast as it warmed in the early 1740s. The only hint I have found of a subsequent history for the statue in Mexico City is a brief news item in the *Gazeta de México* for February 25, 1784, that it was among the images honored with a procession and novena of prayers during the epidemic that winter.[7]

Unlike devotional histories of miraculous images published at the time, much of de la Rosa's account is written in the first person and offers an unusually direct glimpse of the author's devotion to this image of the Virgin Mary and the enthusiasm and trouble his activities caused. It is distinctive also in being more than the vague reminiscence of an elderly priest hurrying to memorialize a defining time of his life and testify to the Virgin Mary's grace before the story was silenced by his death. The level of detail about putative miracles and his own contributions to the image's former popularity—sometimes detailed in ways that make a modern reader wince—is unusual. Attention to detail was second nature to him (his first impulse at Nativitas in 1739 was to size up an armoire in the sacristy for the administrative archive he planned to assemble), but it was also a rhetorical device to establish the text's authority and his own importance. In this it bears comparison to Bernal Díaz del Castillo's account of the Conquest of Mexico, his "True History of the Conquest of New Spain." Both Bernal Díaz and de la Rosa took care to prove themselves trustworthy, almost omniscient eyewitnesses with their wealth of first-hand information. De la Rosa wrote that his account of events and the collections and expenditures on behalf of Nuestra Señora del Patrocinio were based on copious notes he took at the time. He assured the reader that those notes and his personal participation in the events enabled him to be thorough and accurate: "Over the course of nearly three years I saw and experienced the mercies of this sovereign Queen in the way I recount here, without excessive praise or hyperbolic exaggerations." Both he and Bernal Díaz spent some of their twilight years looking back—actively looking, to be sure—on a career in the New World with an epic thread, but less glory and reward than they had hoped for.

Like Bernal Díaz's text, de la Rosa's is a historical account with two perspectives—one very near to the events of 1739–1745, the other retrospective. For the most part it is a straightforward chronological presentation that retains some of the freshness of his experience and observations from the 1730s and 1740s, but with a shift in tone toward the end that underscores the preoccupations driving him to compose it in 1775–1776. He included a copy of the printed image he commissioned to promote the grand celebration and procession of December 1743, placing it in the middle of the manuscript at the point chronologically when it was made and distributed. But it was there as more than documentation or a souvenir. He had commissioned one of the city's finest engravers, Manuel Troncoso, to create the image, and the result was gratifying. As de la Rosa explained, prints from Troncoso's beautiful engraving could themselves become and remain a sacred medium if the devotion to Mary was fervent and sincere. Including this very print. He assured readers at the end of his account in 1776 that a young woman recently recovered from a life-threatening seizure when she prayed to Nuestra Señora del Patrocinio and placed this print on her stomach; and a garbanzo bean that a small boy had stuffed way up his nose popped out when the print was placed on his head just a few days before.

A print from the copper-plate engraving of Our Lady of the Intercession that de la Rosa commissioned. This is the one he included in his manuscript. Courtesy of the Biblioteca Nacional de México, Fondo Reservado. For a larger version of this image, please refer to page 113.

"MY LADY HAS COVERED THE COST OF THE CONSTRUCTION, CONFIRMING HER SPONSORSHIP WITH FREQUENT MIRACLES"

Father de la Rosa's narrative has its mundane side, sprinkled with a bookkeeper's lists of the money, jewels, and building materials collected, the outlays for construction and promotion of the cult of the Virgin during his service in Nativitas, and professional grievances. It contains more autobiography than one would expect to find in a published devotional history of a shrine or prodigious image. But it has in common with published devotional histories a keen interest in providential signs of the Virgin Mary's presence and special favors granted to faithful followers of Nuestra Señora del Patrocinio during the heady days of ardent devotion in the early 1740s. In his enthusiasm, de la Rosa was quick to call them miracles—the term reserved for events that the church hierarchy had certified as supernatural.[8] Building materials mysteriously became available[9]; workers narrowly escaped harm at the construction site, and generous donors and other devotees recovered from illness. He shaped his narrative around these "miracles," much like the official *informaciones jurídicas* compiled in the late sixteenth and seventeenth centuries to establish the authenticity of putative miracles.[10]

The account presents a master list of thirty-five miracles that express his bifocal vision of Nativitas and Mexico City. Most took place in Mexico City or for the benefit of *capitalinos* (twenty-six of his thirty-five events). Individuals recovered their health or were protected from harm in nineteen of the twenty-six Mexico City miracles. Two of the other seven were gifts of building materials. The rest included the recovery of a lost animal, fulfillment of a prediction by a pious nun, an answered prayer to close a gambling house, and two unspecified favors. One-third of the miracles were associated with Troncoso's prints rather than the statue. These miracles extended the reach of the Virgin Mary's mercy to the public places and homes of the weak and poor. Altogether, two-thirds of the individual beneficiaries of her grace were poor people, and most of the remaining third who enjoyed higher social standing and wealth were married women. Altogether, women account for fifteen of the twenty-five miracles for individuals. Were the poor and nominally powerless of Mexico City the most avid believers in the Virgin's mediation and this particular advocation? De la Rosa evinces no interest in the question, but perhaps the printed image of the statue is rare—even though four thousand copies were made and distributed at the time of the rosary procession—because they were well used as devotional objects by the urban poor.[11]

In the presentation of miracles, de la Rosa's gaze turned especially to Mexico City—America's Rome and Jerusalem—home to dozens of shrines and his own hometown; a place replete with distinguished people, patrons, friends, rivals, fellow Franciscans, and divine presence. People of the city were especially deserving of favor, and especially favored, he seemed to say. Repeatedly in his account, important Creole and peninsular Spanish merchants, governors, priests, architects, and other professionals in the capital—or more often their devout wives, sisters, or daughters—asked to have the image brought to them for a day or two. And when they did, good things often followed. They or a relative or servant recovered from serious illness or were saved from harm, and they reciprocated with a generous donation or helped him and his cause in some other way. De la Rosa proved himself a Creole patriot in other writings,[12] and Creole Spaniards and their minions were especially favored in the miracles, but his strong sense of social and racial hierarchy did not simply determine his understanding of who might be worthy of the Virgin's favor.

The two overarching patterns in his presentation of the thirty-five miracles then are (1) Mexico City's favored place in the story and (2) the Virgin Mary's benevolence to her most ardent and self-sacrificing devotees, whatever their race or means.[13] The two patterns converge in his discussion of an explosion in a fireworks factory in the city that touched off a raging fire in 1744. The fire was suddenly extinguished when pious onlookers made way for the statue to be brought forward. He went on to tell of the recovery of a mulato, badly injured in the explosion, who was admitted to a hospital reserved for Spaniards thanks to the Virgin's protection. In his estimation, the man's racial inferiority was overcome by his selfless devotion to Nuestra Señora del Patrocinio and his good reputation in the city, as well as the Virgin's grace. Beyond the idea that America's Rome/Jerusalem and the special protection of the Virgin Mary invited a communion of believers eclipsing social divisions, this incident gave de la Rosa an opportunity to shape his main themes around a pious admonition:

> The most Holy Queen continued to make her presence felt for, once the fire was extinguished and the danger had passed, as I was taking her to the hospital she brought with her a mulato who was wounded all over his body and being carried on a plank. I say that She brought him with her to the hospital, under her protection, because only Spaniards were admitted there, yet his being a mulato was no obstacle in this case because of the respect owed to Most Holy Mary who had just performed a miracle by extinguishing the fire. How could the Sovereign Queen fail to help this mulato who every week gave half a *real* to Fray Agustín Zuleta for the convent's building fund? In all this the friar marveled at the profound judgments of God, as did I. He reported to me that three days before, when he had gone to the fireworks factory to ask for donations for Our Lady, one of the workers rudely responded, "I'll make no donation, father," and this mulato responded, "but I will do it, Father," and took out his half real. Fray Agustín marveled at how Our Lady protected the mulato but not the other man, whose head was smashed by a plank in the devastation done by the fire.[14]

De la Rosa himself seems to have been the most favored of all. A chain of "miracles" kept him safe and well during his mission for Our Lady. He was saved from a kicking mule in the city, from falling debris, from a falling flowerpot, and from a collapsed ladder in Nativitas; he was restored to health from chronic illness; and he found building materials and expert advice when all seemed lost. Perhaps he meant to say that he was just the humble instrument of God's grace and a groundswell of public devotion to Our Lady—protected and favored in order to carry out the work. But a more self-justifying message rises from his text: he was most favored because he was most worthy. We hear repeatedly that thanks to him three thousand *pesos* in money and materials were collected for Our Lady.[15] In effect, he and the Virgin Mary are the protagonists of the story. His text shows no curiosity about Nativitas's experience of the Virgin and the statue before his arrival, or whether his parishioners had their own providential origin story to tell. Rather, the story of the statue begins and ends with him and the miracles he witnessed. It begins with his discovery of a neglected, unattractive image, brought to light, life, and beauty by his efforts, directed by some secret impulse.

"In a highly indecent state thanks to the Indians' neglect"

Father de la Rosa certainly did not think the spiritual impulse propelling these events was coming from his parishioners.[16] On the contrary, he found the Indians of Nativitas ignorant, lazy, truculent, and superstitious. Perhaps in principle they were capable of authentic piety and good works, but not, apparently, without his lead. And they were disinclined to follow.

Indians were little favored by the Virgin in his account of miracles. Most of the nine favors of the Virgin at Nativitas were impersonal and imperfect, not the robust cures and transformations that awaited deserving individuals in Mexico City. It was as if faith in Nativitas was not deep enough to merit more than half-miracles: building materials sometimes became available under mysterious circumstances; a leaning wall did not collapse; no one was seriously injured when a ladder broke; twenty sick Indians survived a typhus epidemic, but some of their children died; a man escaped death in a fall, but suffered lasting injuries; another man lived to tell of being run over by a coach, but he was badly injured; and a pregnant woman survived an especially dangerous birthing with the aid of Our Lady's printed image, but died shortly thereafter at the hands of ignorant Indian midwives.

These dangerous situations often were the Indians' own doing, as when a flowerpot carelessly placed on a ledge by Indian sacristans nearly brained Father de la Rosa; or when two men tumbled off a broken ladder:

> Having made a hole in the face of the wall to hold the head of a supporting beam . . . , a mason was standing on a stepladder, holding one end of the supporting member. At the same time, another

mason was on a flimsier ladder with a crowbar, digging out the
wall where it was to receive the breastwork. The ladder was shaking
as he struck with the tool. Another Indian was on the top rung
of another ladder, supporting the head of the breastwork, while
another one was on the ground raising it with a pole, and another
one was helping with a stout stick. The rest of the Indian laborers
were watching stupidly without offering to help support the base
of the ladder so it would not slip when the mason struck with the
crowbar, so I scolded them and went under the ladder myself.
With both hands, I drew it to my chest. Seeing me do this, a boy
began to climb the ladder instead of staying below. As I called out
to him not to climb up, the ladder I was holding in place broke
apart and the Indian who was using the crowbar, the one who was
supporting the beam, and the breastwork itself all fell straight
toward me. I invoked the Most Holy Virgin as my head, brain,
and spine were about to be struck by the force and weight of the
breastwork. Somehow my body fell outside the wreckage. . . . Only
the blow from falling to the ground hurt me a little on one side.
Neither of those who fell from above landed on top of me, as would
have been natural; nor were they injured.

One exception to the tepid faith and imperfect miracles de la Rosa
associates with Indians is Don Mathías de la Cruz, the Indian sculptor who restored the Nativitas statue. Mathías was a *don*—an Indian
of high status and distinguished lineage—and he was from Tlatelolco,
the famed Indian seat of government within greater Mexico City where
the Franciscans had trained talented Indians for the priesthood in the
sixteenth century. He was "a very good Christian who had a very good
command of the Spanish language." "More than being a very good
Christian (because he did not get drunk), he was very priestly."[17] And
he followed instructions:

The Vicar General contentedly hired him to do the work, giving him
many instructions that every time he took up the carving he was to
invoke the Most Holy Virgin, and when he would work on the face
and hands he had to confess and take communion in honor of the Most
Holy Queen, entrusting his actions to her sponsorship so that an image
would come from his hands as if it had been created by an angel. The
Vicar General's inspired severity made his words so persuasive that the
Indian was greatly moved, promising to confess and take communion
before working on the face and hands of the holy image.

Model Christian that he was, Don Mathías "took refuge in the Most
Holy Virgin" with a heartfelt prayer when his two-year-old son suddenly began to suffocate from a tremendous attack of croup:

He held a lighted candle in his hand, knelt, and, full of faith said to her, "My Lady, you have chosen to emerge so beautifully from my unworthy hands. Please do not let my son die. I have faith that this candle will not go out and that you will return him to me safe and healthy." Great marvel! The Sovereign Queen chose, on one hand, to reward the faith and confidence of the Indian, and on the other to reward the devotion with which he restored her Holy Image. Before the candle went out the child was so free of the dangerous attack that he was safe and healthy again.

Don Mathías is Father de la Rosa's exception that confirms the rule. He is different from every other Indian de la Rosa mentioned during his short and troubled career beyond the archive and library. Whether in Nativitas, Santa María la Redonda, or other pueblos, he was disheartened by what he considered Indians' feeble Christianity and superstitions (which he was inclined to regard as idolatry), and he was often at odds with those he served. Judging by his writings and court appearances, none of the uplifting times in his career had to do with serving Indians. Yet he also wrote of "My poor little ones" and "my zeal to educate Indians in the faith"; and he had dedicated himself to learning Nahuatl, the native language of his parishioners.

Perhaps this paradox of zeal to educate and disdain for the student has as much to do with the Franciscans' view of Indians in the sixteenth century and de la Rosa's sense of a Franciscan tradition in Mexico as it does with the vehemence of his own paternalistic zeal. The proudest time of the Franciscans in Mexico was "the spiritual conquest"—their evangelizing campaign as preachers, teachers, and protectors among Indians in central Mexico during the first decades of Spanish colonization. Millions of Indians became Christians under the guidance of the great heroes of de la Rosa's province—the Apostolic Twelve, Pedro de Gante, and Juan de Zumárraga.[18] In the early debates over the nature of American natives, the Franciscans in Mexico staked out what became the mainstream colonial conception of Indians as children. Early Franciscans rejected both Ginés de Sepúlveda's view of American natives as natural slaves and barely human, and Las Casas's view that they were fully realized humans who lacked only the true religion. Instead, they considered Indians to be young in their humanity and in need of tutelage if they were to reach their human potential. A key difference between de la Rosa and early evangelizers, like Gante and Motolinía, was that they understood Indians-as-children to mean childlike, innocent; their potential to become cultured Christians was great. Two centuries later, de la Rosa could not shake off his conviction that Indians were childish rather than childlike—disobedient mischief-makers, if not devious idolaters in the devil's clutches. He wanted to inspire the multitude; he had too little of the steadying patience and forgiveness to teach to the few. In his way, de la Rosa understood that he hoped for a grander mission than that of a family doctor of Indian souls.

Would the people of Nativitas have agreed with these stories of miracles, troublesome Indians, and service to the Virgin Mary? Not likely, but there is no record of the providential stories they told then. That they were more devoted to the Virgin, the liturgy, and the religious life of their community than he acknowledged is more certain; and their devotional practices and store of sacred things were more numerous and varied than he described in his narrative about this one image. He knew this well enough judging by the detailed lists of the church's possessions he compiled at Nativitas and the earlier inventories he found among the church papers. The inventories of the sacristy and church from 1718 to 1738 document that Nativitas had a full supply of vestments, silver chalices, candleholders, altar cloths, and other liturgical items. In addition to the main altar dedicated to the Virgin Mary, the church boasted altars to Christ, Joseph, the Virgin of Guadalupe, Souls in Purgatory, San Diego, Our Lady of the Rosary, Our Lady of Sorrows and the Holy Sepulchre, and Our Lady of the Rosary.[19]

The report on moveable property in the Nativitas church written shortly before Father de la Rosa first went there noted that some of the liturgical items were old and needed repair. It also warned the Indian sacristans not to lend anything to the subject village of San Simón for their Palm Sunday festivities and not to pawn precious things from the sacristy in the local taverns. Even so, the church of Nativitas was better furnished than he acknowledged in his text, both before his arrival and after his departure, and the Virgin Mary in several representations had long been the central devotional figure in this doctrina named in honor of the Nativity of the Virgin.[20] Although the image of the Virgin Mary was not beautiful to his eye before it was restored, this opinion was not universal and the people of Nativitas had not neglected it. It was there on the main altar in 1690, described by the Franciscan pastor as "exceedingly beautiful" (de peregrina hermosura),[21] nearly fifty years before Father de la Rosa's time. His own inventory of jewels and other precious belongings of Our Lady in 1739 included a gold-plated silver "imperial crown" and a chain of fifty-nine French coins that were placed over the shoulders and hands of the statue "when they took it out on procession and showered it with confetti."[22]

Even in de la Rosa's text the people of Nativitas honored the Virgin more than one would expect from his statements about their indifference and dirty hands. They contributed thirty pesos for the restoration of the statue and received the beautified image with great rejoicing. Leaders of the community stood guard whenever the image traveled to Mexico City at their pastor's frequent urging,[23] and they moved the lumber and stone for the construction projects and did most of the work on site. He thought they were careless stewards of the coveted statue and little church, but both the statue and the church were there long after he left. In 1807, with the backing of the Indian governor of Mexico City's Parcialidad de San Juan, the parish priest, and the *provisor de indios* (the archbishop's administrator for Indian affairs), leaders of Nativitas gained permission to collect alms in order to rebuild the church from its foundations. The old structure was, again, much deteriorated and they wanted it to be "decente" (proper).[24] The community alms collector at the time referred to the wonder-working image as Nuestra Señora de Nativitas, not the Nuestra Señora del Patrocinio of de la Rosa's text.[25]

Nativitas in the eighteenth century is less accessible to historians than Father de la Rosa's views and activities thanks to his long paper trail, but it was not as fixed and featureless a place as he seemed to suggest. Both de la Rosa and people of Nativitas may have regarded the pueblo and the capital as separate worlds, but Nativitas was almost as much a part of Mexico City as de la Rosa himself was. People of Nativitas had taken up residence in the city, without losing their ties to their pueblo a three-hour walk away. Their economic activities—brickmaking, haymaking, salt and saltpeter processing—were directed to the urban market and routinely took local people there on business.[26]

De la Rosa would pay a price for thinking of Nativitas as a timeless place apart and underestimating his parishioners' political connections in the city and their appetite for litigation. There was, for example, more to the pueblo's invitation to the governor and other dignitaries of the Indian district of San Juan to celebrate the return of the refurbished statue than the angelic voices of the cantors they brought along.[27] As Joseph Vásquez, the newly appointed royal lieutenant for the Nativitas area would learn in late 1739, the elders of Nativitas looked to the governor of San Juan and the chief judge of the Audiencia of Mexico as their political patrons and authorities, and would resist direction from other officials. The dispute over their resistance to Vásquez's authority and what he called "the violent deaths and other grave excesses committed outside the city," dragged on through most of de la Rosa's time in Nativitas, yet he seems to have missed its implications for his own contingent authority.[28] He would recognize too late that he could not simply have his way in Nativitas.

CONCLUSION

At one level, Father de la Rosa's ambitions and career retrace the sixteenth-century history of Franciscans in Mexico—from an expansive, evangelizing zeal and some freedom to act upon it; to intervention by superiors; to conflict, withdrawal, and disappointment over the interference and incomplete results; to a longing for renewal. But these were not neat, sequential stages in de la Rosa's life, and there are other differences that have much to do with this friar and his time.

Like the founding generation, he was a doer more than a thinker, a self-described man of "ardent zeal" focused on the idea of spiritual revival and conquest. But he was a less independent, less imposing figure than such famous predecessors as Pedro de Gante, Motolinía, and Martín de Valencia. He was a weaker character ensnared in the institutional life of the order and the politics of a different time, a city man much attached to his role as an occasional notary and inspector of books for the Inquisition.[29] He could care more about his personal dignity and reputation than was fitting for a mendicant (memorably here when he abandoned a "ridiculous mule" at the entrance to the city rather than be seen collecting alms in such an "indecent" manner[30]). Above all, his idea of evangelizing mission was clouded by his Mexico City preoccupations and his low opinion of Indians as fellow Christians. He seems to have been happiest and most effective amid stacks of documents, conducting the business of the archive and library. There his punctiliousness, energy, and talent for managing records and ordering facts made him invaluable to the Franciscans in the years of litigation for the order that followed his removal from Nativitas.[31]

The years spanned by de la Rosa's association with the image of Nuestra Señora del Patrocinio (1739–1775) were momentous for the institutional church and local religion in the viceroyalty, and it was an especially trying period for the Franciscans. Royal officials and regalist bishops were moving to curb "excessive" popular devotions and the influence of friar-pastors. They decreed fewer and less elaborate feast day celebrations, challenged the use of Indian languages in the liturgy, virtually removed the mendicant orders from their traditional pastoral responsibilities in central and southern Mexico, and limited the authority of parish priests in other ways.[32] Between 1749 and the time he composed his account of Nuestra Señora del Patrocinio, the Franciscans lost nearly all of their doctrinas (including Nativitas), and other reforms to further professionalize and subordinate the clergy were well under way.

De la Rosa was alert to these changes, especially during his years in charge of the archive and library,[33] and he was an avid student of early

Franciscan history in Mexico. But he was blind to patterns of a less remote past and how his own troubles folded into the higher politics of church and state that swirled around him. He was convinced that his troubles at Nativitas and elsewhere—including his failure to win a place among the Fernandines, the string of reassignments, and his eventual removal from pastoral service—had to do with fickle Indians and the vagaries of personal patronage and opinion. He was certain that a lone dissenting Fernandine, a new Franciscan provincial who arbitrarily took the Indians' side, and the retirement of his friend and patron Antonio Ramírez del Castillo as vicar general of the Archdiocese of Mexico caused his misfortunes. His account gives no inkling that aggressive promotion of Nuestra Señora del Patrocinio, loose talk of miracles, impolitic criticism of colonial authorities, impatience with parishioners, and thirst for the glory of a distant past might be considered excessive, even dangerous, by archbishops, audiencias, viceroys, and Franciscan superiors of his time. And he was surprisingly unconcerned by (if he was aware of) the many times a pastor's "improving," replacing, or merely moving a religious image to a different place in the church led to angry commotions, bloodshed, and litigation with Indian parishioners in central Mexico during the seventeenth and eighteenth centuries. Whereas de la Rosa's idea of a fitting devotion kept drawing him and the statue back to the city,[34] it is not surprising that people of Nativitas wanted the Virgin Mary to work her wonders at home as the fame of their image spread.

De la Rosa had been careful to obtain Archbishop Vizarrón's permission to organize the rosary procession in the city and gain an indulgence from him for the participants. Nevertheless, this longtime archbishop (1731–1747), who also served as viceroy from 1734–1740, was, in the long run, bound to take a dim view of this kind of popular euphoria. Was it just whim on the part of de la Rosa's provincial and the Indians of Nativitas that ended the statue's visits to the city? Was it mere coincidence that a month after he was removed from Nativitas in 1745 the archbishop closed the shrine of Nuestra Señora de los Angeles at Tlaltelolco because it attracted disorderly crowds? These were not de la Rosa's questions, but Archbishop Vizarrón had good reasons to cool off an overheated pastor and tranquilize many of the Marian devotions that had gained popularity in the Valley of Mexico in the wake of the great epidemic of 1737. Vizarrón's conviction that devotion to Our Lady of Guadalupe had saved Mexico City in 1737 led him to promote Guadalupe as patroness of the city and viceroyalty and to pursue a campaign in Rome for official papal recognition (which came in 1754, after Vizarrón's death). Promoting one image as the dominant symbol of identity and protection for New Spain and its capital city fitted the regalist program of centralizing and standardizing devotional practices, and de la Rosa's Franciscan superiors had more pressing battles to fight than the cult of Nuestra Señora del Patrocinio. They must have been concerned by his persistent problems in Nativitas and his dreamy vision of a return to the sixteenth century as they struggled to convince eighteenth-century royal governors and archbishops of their order's importance to the future of crown and church in New Spain.

Father de la Rosa's vivid account of the wonders of Nuestra Señora del Patrocinio stood out from the run of routine administrative papers I had been reading in the archive of the Province of the Holy Gospel. Only later did I recognize that his mark was everywhere in this colonial archive. He had been through all of these documents before me, poring over their contents, putting them in order, filling in gaps, and writing explanatory notes here and there. How this archive became his—how it was an extension of his longtime aspirations as a Franciscan—took me by surprise when I began to find his tracks in other archives and libraries in Mexico City, Austin, Berkeley, and Chicago. Some of the records that surfaced were pieces of an ambitious project he undertook single-handedly late in life to identify and catalogue all the Franciscans of his province beginning with the first group of twelve in 1523. Compiled between 1760 and 1770, the principal item is a 483-page "Bezerro general menológico y chronológico de todos los religiosos que ha avido en la Provincia." Meaning a register of saints with brief biographies of each one, the term "menológico" suggests his commemorative purpose and the epic terms in which he saw the history of his province, especially in its early years. At the time he made his last entry, more than 5,200 deceased members had been entered. Each is classified alphabetically under the first letter of his surname, then chronologically by date of profession. Work on this elaborately cross-indexed catalogue of the membership and related inquiries into the accomplishments of his predecessors "cost me a tremendous effort . . . which consumed many years of work," he wrote in his sometimes over-the-top way.[35]

He had been removed from his post at Nativitas, prevented from actively continuing his Marian mission, and left with less exalted (if not unimportant) duties that kept him out of circulation. But he was not broken by the experience or left in a state of suspended animation; nor, to all appearances, was he embittered. Here in the various indexes he compiled and the archive of the Province of the Holy Gospel, as well as in his many unpublished writings,[36] was evidence of a busy, purposeful life within cloistered walls. His consuming passion for lists and good order, his new, more restricted circumstances, the troubling political changes then facing the Franciscans in Mexico, and his hankering after transcendent service turned him toward the history of his province's work in Mexico. It was a history he found liberally sprinkled with miracles and exemplary evangelizers. This work of preserving and in some sense reliving the collective history of his province led him back to his own exalted time at Nativitas and forward to the composition of his account of the miracles of Nuestra Señora del Patrocinio and thoughts of revival.

The little church with one bell tower is still there in the parish of Nativitas, facing a noisy eight-lane thoroughfare between the Viaducto de la Piedad and Eje 5, no longer beyond the city limits. A rectangular stone high on the front wall is dated 1563, but there has been extensive reconstruction, and not only under Father de la Rosa's busy direction.[37] The statue of Our Lady displayed at the altar could well be the one restored, revered, and promoted by Father de la Rosa. It is draped in a fresh cloak, its hair renewed and restyled, its painted surfaces in fine condition. His title for the statue—Nuestra Señora del Patrocinio, Our Lady of Intercession—has been forgotten. It is known only as Nuestra Señora de Nativitas. The origin story parishioners tell underscores the statue's providential attachment to this place, without a hint of its travels and fame in the city during the eighteenth century. As the story goes, when the image was being taken from the hospital village of Santa Fe long ago in the sixteenth century, it became irresistibly heavy there at Nativitas and could not be moved further. Local people heeded this sign from Our Lady and built a chapel on the site to house the image. Once a year, during the *fiesta patronal* in September, the image is carried through the streets that trace the parish limits. The privilege of sponsoring the fiesta is reserved for the old families of the neighborhood that have not moved away.[38]

Document

History of Miracles Worked by the Image of Our Lady of Intercession which is Venerated in the Monastery of Nativitas of Tepetlatzinco Pueblo, by Fray Francisco de la Rosa Figueroa (1776)

[p. 1]

No. 1. For the honor and glory of God Our Lord and his Most Holy Mother in her most miraculous image of Our Lady of Intercession,[1] venerated in the monastery of Nativitas de México, pueblo of Tepetlatzinco, I, Fray Francisco Antonio de la Rosa Figueroa, General Preacher, Apostolic Notary and notary for the Inquisition, Inspector of Books, and Archivist of this Sacred Province of the Holy Gospel, have undertaken in this year of 1775 to write a clean version of the history of the manifest miracles and marvels that I experienced during the rebuilding of that little monastery, undertaken in obedience to my superiors, from the beginning of 1743 during the Very Reverend Father Fray Manuel Enciso's term as provincial to the end of 1745 when Our Father Fray Bernardo de Arratia was provincial. I copy this history from notebooks I kept then and later copied during 1755 as Archivist of this Holy Province in order to leave an account in the archive should later chroniclers among the Reverend Fathers wish to make use of them to preserve the memory of this Most Holy Image and the little monastery which belonged to this Province until 1770 when the Archbishop's office secularized it. During the course of almost three years I saw and experienced the mercies of this Sovereign Queen in the manner I speak of here without excessive praise or hyperbolical exaggerations. I would not dare to judge them hyperboles even once if what I say were not true.

No. 2. And because at the time I only bothered to jot down the miracles I witnessed during the rebuilding of the little monastery when I was placed there a second time by Our Very Reverend Father and Commissary Fray Pedro Navarrete, I shall reduce them to this narrative in order to make manifest the ways Divine Providence confused my plans and those of my superiors and arranged and commanded, to my confusion and to the benefit of the cult of the Sovereign Queen, that the same superior prelate who put that ministry under my charge for the first time in 1739 would place me there again in 1743. I have already described in notebook 16 of this file beginning at paragraph 12 the unprecedented commotion at the inauguration of the Third Order of St. Francis in Cuernavaca caused by the mission made by the fathers of the Colegio de San Fernando. This mission in 1735 so startled my [p. 2] spirit and so moved my inclination to the missionary's life that I immediately decided to seek a way to leave the ministry among Indians and proceed to the Colegio de San Fernando. With permission from the Provincial, Our Father Leozquera, I went as a candidate to that *colegio*,[2] where the fathers welcomed me into their community, hoping that I would join them in order to missionize in Indian pueblos and teach the Mexican language to some fathers. But after a month, during which I hoped to become a member, the venerable council of the colegio, by secret vote, decided not to admit me because one important father was opposed. Since I did not achieve my desire, and had been approved two years before in the Synod of Pastors, I anticipated that I would be appointed the chief minister in a curacy or would continue ministering to Indians, so I returned to this main monastery.[3] From there, Our Father Pérez sent me to the curacy of Calimaya the next year; that is, the beginning of 1737. There I learned of the utter poverty and helplessness of my aged father far from home in Zacatecas where, having become a miner, he lost his fortune. He was deeply in debt and completely without resources, and I was unable to bring him to me, even to pay for his trip, so I had to prevail upon Our Father Terreros, Guardian of the Colegio de San Fernando, to intercede by letter with the Reverend Father Guardian of the Colegio de Zacatecas secretly to arrange for my father to join me. This was in order to avoid his arrest for nonpayment of tributes because, having twice been alcalde mayor and received special praise from two viceroys, the second time (because he was a very simple-hearted man) he received the tribute payments in cloth from the Sierra, went to sell it in Zacatecas, bought the mine with the money, and lost it all. In the meantime I was reassigned from the curacy of Calimaya to that of Mazatepec in the district of Cuernavaca, where my father joined me. Appointed and honored by viceroys and other illustrious persons, he was now so destitute that I had to go into debt in Cuernavaca just to clothe him with minimal decency. Learning this, Our Very Reverend Father Navarrete placed me, during the interim meeting of January 31,

1739, for the first time as chief minister of the monastery of Nativitas, where my father accompanied me. I have related my cares because through them I pondered in the secrecy of my heart how God had taken notice of them to have the Superior Prelate appoint me to the poor little monastery of the Most Holy Virgin so that my sinfulness could promote her cult and the veneration of her most miraculous image, as I shall describe below.

[p. 3]

No. 3. I entered that monastery in the company of Father Fray Joseph Villa, taking my father with me; but in coming to recognize the deplorable condition of the residence, church, sacristy, and little cloister, only God knows how distressed I was. The residence had five cells above, including the principal one, erected over the old walls that corresponded to the basement below, which served as the original living quarters. The little cloister seemed suspended in air; the church and sacristy were crumbling; the walls were ruined by saltpeter deposits; the holy things in the church, sacristy, and ornaments of the altar were in a highly indecent state thanks to the Indians' neglect; the lower rooms did not correspond to the inventory; and the written rules and instructions were as full of blemishes and erasures as the inventory. The clerical fees were so meager that they could not fully support a single friar, much less two even with a weekly ration of only seven pesos, not to mention the salary and maintenance of a cook, plus the other expenses and contributions including the triannual contribution to the province, the provisioning of the monastery, and the services of the infirmary. Thinking about all of this made my blood freeze. It was even more unsettling to discover that the residence was about to collapse because the lower basement was crumbling from saltpeter. Only God gave me the spirit to devise ways to repair as far as possible the imminent threats to the residence, the ruinous state of the sacred paraphernalia, the great indecency with which the Indians treated the things of the sacristy and, most lamentable of all, the Most Holy Image of Our Lady. I will only say here, in order not to elaborate unduly, that at the cost of embarrassing myself with my benefactors, alms from masses I undertook, and frequent sermons and shifts of work during Lent in this city between 1739 and 1740, you will be astonished to find in the folio inventory book I fashioned, in file 58 of this archive, that my collections for the sacred paraphernalia and repairs to the monastery exceeded 3,000 pesos. Here I must add that this inventory and the order from the superior prelate which is on page 108 negate Father Fray Joseph Herrera's absurdity—he, choosing not to appreciate the clarity of my aforesaid inventory which was fully authorized by the superior prelates in the proceedings of the pastoral visits which follow p. 108, requested a new inventory from Our Father Ximeno on the pretext that mine was confusing. But he missed a little inventory included there, undoubtedly done in 1770 when the church and monastery were turned over to the archdiocese, which the priest who assumed office there would have overlooked. By comparing the two, one can identify everything that Father Herrera did not see or which was lost and used up during the twenty-five years the property was in the Indians' possession. I had sought to prevent such a decline as soon as I entered for the first time and informed myself about what there was and what was not included in the little old inventory by recording everything I found there, as will be seen from folios 28 to 38, which I later copied in my aforesaid inventory. And to show that my ardent desire was to provide relief for the monastery, for the priest in residence, and for the Indians themselves, I refer the reader to the directory I drew up which will be found in box 55 entitled Directories, file 3, no. 30. And if I elaborated at length in my inventory [p. 4], it was on the one hand to instruct and facilitate the work of my successors by providing the most important knowledge and advice—there is not a wasted word in it—and on the other hand to leave a most exact inventory of everything I received upon arrival and to distinguish clearly all that I added and repaired throughout the compound during my first assignment there in 1739 and 1740, and the repairs I undertook as far as I could in the monastery. These were not as extensive as I wished because much money was needed and I neither had the means to obtain it nor could the people help me because of their poverty, which grew worse among the families that lost members during the recent devastation caused by the *matlazahuatl* epidemic.

No. 4. But God, who arranges everything sweetly and strongly, arranged for a better time the ways and means that I missed and that would produce devotion and glory for the Most Holy Virgin. At the end of Lent at the beginning of April 1739 Joseph Ramírez del Castillo, *cura*[4] of the Cathedral and Vicar General for Indian affairs, to whom I owed many frequent kindnesses of a father and very intimate friend, took great pains on my behalf to favor the Indians and console me in my difficulties. Once when he went to visit me he saw the miserable condition of the monastery as well as the efforts I had undertaken to make possible repairs. Noticing the little devotion evoked by the condition of the Most Holy Patroness, because it was an old carving and its face and hands were ugly and out of proportion, he was moved (undoubtedly by the Most Holy Virgin) to say to me with all conviction that this image should be restored and refined with the greatest skill. He said he knew a renowned and reliable craftsman in the parish of Tlaltelolco—a sculptor, altar maker, and gilder. He awakened the Indians of the pueblo to the undertaking and they responded enthusiastically. With my help and that of the Vicar General they collected thirty pesos. He told them to cover the holy image and bring it to his house. This was sometime during that same month of April. He sent for his friend the Indian sculptor, who was very fluent in Spanish; and more than being a good Christian (because he did not get drunk) he was very priestly. The Vicar General contentedly hired him to do the work, giving him many instructions that every time he took up the carving he was to invoke the Most Holy Virgin, and when he would work on the face and hands he had to confess and take communion in honor of the Most Holy Queen, entrusting his actions to her sponsorship so that an image would come from his hands as if it had been created by an angel. The Vicar General's inspired severity made his words so persuasive that the Indian was greatly moved, promising to confess and take communion before working on the face and hands of the holy image. The Indians of the pueblo took the sacred sculpture from the home of the Vicar General and carried it covered to Tlaltelolco, to the house of the good Indian. While he was working on it I dedicated myself to the good order, embellishment, and majesty of the new *sacrarium*⁵ and main altar, as my inventory records from folio 60 to 61.

No. 5. At the end of June of the same year the Most Holy Image was restored, transformed into a sacred lodestone of hearts. To bring it from the sculptor's house I arranged for the Indians of Nativitas to carry to the said house the portable platform of the Holy Sepulcher so the image could be carried lying flat, face up, well protected against dust, and protecting the face to make sure that her eyelashes would not come unglued. In this manner they brought it directly to the Vicar General's house where it was placed standing on a table that served as an altar. This gentleman delighted in its beauty, unable to stop looking at it and admiring it. During the following days I devised a stand on which to transport it [p. 5] that would make it very solid and secure on the litter or little baldachin,⁶ with screws and little iron doors on the four sides plus two latches and a square oak support almost half a *vara*⁷ long that crossed the little baldachin and secured the stand on which this most beautiful image was placed. The only thing lacking (said the Vicar General) was a setting worthy of its beauty. At this point I took the opportunity to ask his permission to have it remain in Mexico City, to be taken to various houses that I enumerated and the convents of nuns rather than carried back to the pueblo for the

September feast day, because if it were taken there and then brought back, there would be the danger that it would be dropped on the way. Also, once it was in its niche the pueblo would oppose letting it be taken to Mexico City. The Vicar General answered me that my plans seemed very good and that I should not worry about the second eventuality because he would dissuade the Indians. He thought I might be able to collect very good alms. He also told me to have the Indian officials sent to him on his orders and that in my presence he would overcome whatever difficulties there might be. When they did appear before him he exhorted them with a talk that was very sweet and very much in favor of my plans. They left very contented, all the more so when I begged the Vicar General to come bless this beautiful, Most Holy Image and the new sacrarium, and authorize the titular feast in the presence of the Holy Sacrament before the beginning of Lent. He promised me that he would do so and they left very pleased and grateful; so, whenever I came to Mexico City to take the Most Holy Image from one place to another the *alcaldes*[8] assigned me four or more Indians to do it. I attribute all of these decisions, actions, and plans by the Vicar General and me to the Sovereign Queen. By these means her miraculous image began to be known in Mexico City, allowing me to enlarge her cult in her temple, refurbish the sacristy, and obtain funds with which to repair, as far as possible, the threats to the residence described above. Of all of this I presented to the Very Reverend Provincial Syndic[9] in July 1740 a brief account of the more than 3,000 pesos that were collected.

No. 6. On January 20, 1740, I decided to take the sovereign image to its temple, covered and with the greatest care, mounted on its stand so that the wind would not damage it in transit. It was beautifully attired and adorned with all the gold jewelry and pearls that had been donated to her, and a beautiful little wig. And once the pueblo heard that the image was on the way the commotion was great and young and old made ready the salvo of rockets, bombs, and tolling of bells with which they received the Most Holy Patroness, congratulating one other and me for having made possible, with the help of the Vicar General, the presence in the church of their pueblo such a beautiful image as their patroness. Meanwhile I put it in the main part of the church (putting the Blessed Sacrament on another altar) while I proceeded to arrange the new sacrarium and the niche in which to place it. This was done quickly, and once it was in place I made ready for the titular feast on February 7 with the greatest solemnity I could muster because the Vicar General was going to bless [p. 6] the Most Holy Image and the new sacrarium for the Blessed Sacrament and

authorize the feast day. For this event I invited Don Domingo del
Campo, the gunpowder supplier, to act as godfather for the blessing,
and he gave me a donation for the cult of the Most Holy Virgin. For
the ceremony at the altar I requested friars. The Indians invited the
governor of San Juan and his officials, who brought good cantors, and
I preached the sermon in the presence of the Blessed Sacrament. This
is recorded in number 26 of my volume in praise of Mary among the
five volumes I leave bound and marked with the seal of this library.
From this day on I found the Indians more docile and very devoted
to the Most Holy Virgin, while the Vicar General became ever kinder
in favoring me. To this point I have recounted the events of 1739 and
1740 that I neglected to set down in 1745 and 1755. As I said at the
beginning this was because my intention in my notes was only to set
down the miracles of the Most Holy Virgin as I saw and experienced
them in 1743–1744.

No. 7. The year 1739. Before recounting the events that God
ordained for my second appointment to that monastery, this is the
appropriate place to write down the first manifest miracle that the
Sovereign Queen worked through her restored image on behalf of the
same artisan who restored it. This man was named Don Mathías de
la Cruz, a very good Christian who had a very good command of the
Spanish language. Having followed the instructions and advice given
to him by the Vicar General for the success of the restoration of the
most beautiful image and completed the work, his little two-year-old
son was close to dying from a sudden and tremendous attack of croup,
suffocating because in that urgent moment a timely remedy was not at
hand. He took refuge in the Most Holy Virgin, lit a candle in his hand,
knelt, and, full of faith, appealed to her, "My Lady, you have chosen to
emerge so beautifully from my unworthy hands. Please do not let my
son die. I have faith that this candle will not go out and that you will
return him to me safe and healthy." Great marvel! The Sovereign Queen
chose, on one hand to reward the faith and confidence of the Indian, and
on the other to reward the devotion with which he restored her Holy
Image: before the candle went out the child was so free of the dangerous
attack that he was safe and healthy again. The said Mathías told me all
of this with great tenderness, and I swear to it *in verbo sacerdotis*.[10]

No. 8. From here on I will make manifest the ways in which Divine
Providence diverted the prelates' plans, confusing me in my baseness
by having the superior prelate who removed me from the monastery
of Nativitas in 1740 send me back in 1743 for the rebuilding and to
make known throughout Mexico City the most beautiful image of Our
Lady of Intercession. In view of the account of the funds totaling more

than 3,000 pesos [p. 7] free and clear added by me to the poor little monastery of Nativitas that I submitted in July 1740, in which month Our Father Suárez was elected Provincial, Our Very Reverend Father Navarrete decided that for me to have more income for the support of my poor father who accompanied me, I should be transferred to the curacy of Xochitepec in the district of Cuernavaca which was richer although its pueblos and sugar mills were more difficult to administer. It was Father Navarrete who gave me the friar's habit during his first term as Provincial, and during the second showed great confidence in my meager abilities, which he continued to show throughout the time he was Commissary General. With a great show of affection and confidence he supported my zeal to educate Indians in the faith, even persisting with the king's attorney general for a favorable result in the matter of an official writ against the Indians of Tepepam.

But I had only served eleven months as an assistant there when Our Father Fray Diego Suárez sent me a very official letter ordering me to come obediently to Mexico City to take possession of the curacy of Santa María la Redonda. He added that I was in no way to resist the appointment because the viceroy had already chosen me, that I was to come immediately, leaving the monastery in its present condition to one of my companions there, the Father and General Preacher Fray Juan Pérez Conde. The weight I felt at such a sudden transfer was very great; first because during the eight years since my certification for pastoral duty I had fled from such an appointment; second, because I owed the Syndic, Don Joseph Días Leal, 100 pesos for the sacrarium in the Nativitas church; and third, because I supposed that my election as cura, which the prelate's letter pressed, was the work of Our Father Navarrete who was thinking about my security and my ability to support my father decently. So I obeyed Our Father Suárez's wishes, although humbly expressing my distaste for a curacy; but the Reverend Father again enjoined me to obey. So as not to resist I took possession on August 30, 1741, extremely dejected at the prospect of being unable to return to the monastery of Nativitas to act on my yearning to build a new monastery and church in tribute to the beauty of the Most Holy Image of my Lady. My dejection grew when I learned from Father Guardian Fray Diego de Hinojosa that he, without knowing my wishes, was the one who had interceded with Our Very Reverend Father Navarrete and the Reverend Father Provincial to make me cura in order to bring the Indians of that curacy under control. (They are particularly indomitable, as my petition to Viceroy Conde de Fuenclara shows, advising him that if the situation did not improve, I would resign the curacy. This brief will be found in box 93, file 3, part 2, no. 17.) Father Hinojosa's second ardent desire was that I would help him with the building of the dressing room under construction for Our Lady and the rebuilding of that temple because he knew of the substantial funds I had raised through my benefactors to alleviate the poverty of the Nativitas monastery. As for controlling the Indians [of Santa María la Redonda], the year and a half I devoted to working, preaching, and punishing them had no effect. I tried every means that prudence dictated and used all the resources and strategies I could think of. At the urging of the Vicar General I went to every court of law showing that of the 3,000 parishioners registered in the parish censuses, barely 300 accepted my authority. I endured this until my health was broken and I could no longer perform the duties of the office. Then I asked the Most Illustrious and Most Excellent Archbishop Vizarrón to accept my resignation from the curacy. His Most Illustrious Excellency resisted because I owed him special affection and singular devotion and favor, as indicated by the copy of the order he issued as viceroy on my behalf in 1734 against the Indians of Tepepam, which is filed in this archive in box 93, file 3, part I, no. 11.

His Highness's reason for resisting [p. 8] my proposed resignation (as I said above) was because he thought that my superiors were forcing me to resign. I learned that his Most Illustrious Excellency had ordered a secret investigation about this. I shall drop this point now in order to demonstrate the ways that God's Providence not only facilitated the Archbishop's change of heart, but led Our Very Reverend Father Navarrete to carry my resignation of the curacy to conclusion and, in the next provincial chapter meeting, to appoint me for a second time to that little monastery which only by a miracle had not collapsed, as one can infer below.

No. 9. Father Hinojosa's second ardent desire for me was that as pastor of Santa María I would obtain donations for the rebuilding of that temple, but it came to naught because the many times I planned to approach one or another of my benefactors I forgot or was distracted by the thought and the great want and danger of collapse of the Nativitas monastery. Having nothing else on my mind, I replied to myself privately, alone, saying why should I be working for the benefit of this temple if the guardian has the funds for this project with the donations he collects? Would it not be better to reserve these efforts for that poor little monastery that is about to collapse and needs them more? But how can I rejoin that curacy? What will my superiors say of me? And, should they allow me to resign, will the Archbishop accept my resignation? And, should they accept it, will I be able to return to that monastery? And how can I face Our Father Commissary with such a petition? Most Holy Virgin, you know why it suits me to leave this curacy. If you do so and you take me to your little monastery, I promise to do everything I can to build you a church, altarpiece, and monastery. But how? It would be madness for me to undertake such a project, but didn't I raise more than 3,000 pesos before? Didn't God himself help me then? Why, then, am I doubtful? I must throw myself into every effort to return to that monastery, which is about to collapse. All of this happened in the secrecy of my heart, and in my notes I swore to it in verbo sacerdotis. And the Sovereign Queen smoothed away all the difficulties, providing as an instrument of my consolation that I should visit the home of a distinguished family and chat with the wife of Don Juan de Lexarzar. He was a close friend of Our Father Navarrete, who visited this lady and deeply loved their young daughters. I was the daughters' confessor and the whole family loved me very much. In the daughters' presence I unburdened myself to this lady of all my cares concerning the matters mentioned above. After hearing me, this lady granted me her wholehearted support in convincing Our Very Reverend Father Navarrete before the next chapter meeting to accept my resignation of the curacy and return me to the Nativitas monastery. She was certain she would succeed by sending one of her daughters to plead with the Very Reverend Father. This daughter asked me for a little slip of paper noting what I sought for my consolation. On it I laid out my entreaty: that the Very Reverend Father allow me to resign the curacy [p. 9] before the Archbishop, that the chapter allow me to return to Nativitas, and that, if I were allowed to return, I promised to remake the monastery and even the church. The girl was so eager that she neglected to memorize my petition and simply put my slip of paper in the prelate's hands, which left me extremely perplexed. But I achieved it all, and with his consent I resigned the curacy, guarding against the disapproval of the Archbishop by accompanying my resignation with medical certifications of the illnesses I had contracted in that curacy bestowed upon me in obedience to my superiors. Then the provincial chapter meeting convened by Our Father Enciso took place and on February 17, 1743, and they announced my appointment for a second time as assistant in the monastery of Nativitas.

No. 10. As soon as I took possession of the monastery my predecessor, Fray Roque Santa Ana, who knew I was his successor, received me crying gently and telling me that he thanked God heartily for sending me to save that monastery from its imminent danger of collapsing, which he had not been able to remedy because of his consummate poverty and great illnesses, for he could hardly take a step without feeling faint. Alarmed by this news, I found myself again

amidst the great poverty of which I had freed the curacy, deprived
of everything, for I arrived on a borrowed horse with my poor father.
Resolving not to postpone the remedy, I took the opportunity to visit
the master builder of the cathedral and the viceregal palace, and
Don Manuel Alvares, master builder for the city, and asked them to
donate their services for an inspection of the monastery and church
and give me a certification in writing as to the dangers therein to
present to my superiors. The inspectors confirmed my impressions,
which I have already made manifest. They (and later the masons
and Indians of the pueblo) marveled that only by a miracle was the
monastery still standing; for, not only was the entire adobe structure
very large and laced with saltpeter, and the sloping face of the walls
made of stone and earth, and the construction much older than the
1653 rebuilding of the church over the old monastery that was below,
but all of the walls were almost half a vara out of line, some leaning in,
others leaning out, with the greatest threat to the supporting walls. The
heads of the timbers of the terrace roofs were rotten where they were
covered with plaster, as were the crossbeams, so that with the great
weight of over half a vara of earth and above that, brick, it was only by
a miracle that the crossbeams had not collapsed. This was discovered
more precisely during the inspection that the masons later made of the
roofs. Where I had reroofed in 1739, thinking the danger most urgent,
it was evident when they removed the roof in 1743 that the timbers
that seemed sound could be pulled out with one blow upwards as
easily as if they were touchwood, so rotten were they. I swore to all
of this in verbo sacerdotis in my first notes [p. 10] as an eyewitness,
marveling at the protection of the Sovereign Queen of Intercession,
without which the monastery would have collapsed under the weight
of the roofs and leaning walls over the sloping faces and decayed
foundations that were swollen and ruined by saltpeter all around,
some by a quarter of a vara, some by half a vara. Only by a miracle was
the residence standing, as if suspended in air. All of this the best master
builders certified for me in writing, testifying that if it was not shored
up soon the monastery threatened to fall to ruins before anything more
was spent on it.

No. 11. I went with this certification to Our Very Reverend Father
Navarrete. He thanked me for this prompt guidance and approved my
decision. I went on to Our Father Enciso. I advised him of my plans
to seek donations of old lumber in all of Mexico City's construction
sites in order to shore up the entire monastery. My decision greatly
pleased the Reverend Father, and when I told him that I only felt
afflicted by my lack of a mount—for in order to come to Mexico City

I borrowed such a ridiculous mule and saddle from someone who rents them that I left them with the guards at the city gate so as not to enter on this animal—the Reverend Father freely granted me his own well-equipped mule, giving me a letter to send for it. I attribute this to God's will, for with this mule I soon acquired not only all the necessary lumber by donation, but I was able to collect substantial donations for the construction and sacred paraphernalia. I number among the miracles that Most Holy Mary performed for my benefit that, having entered that monastery sick with intermittent fevers and arthritic pains (as the physicians certified to the Archbishop for my resignation from the curacy), and working so much and so continuously, flushed with the effort, I experienced neither fever nor even a slight headache.

No. 12. The entire monastery was shored up thanks to miracles that will be noted as briefly as possible. I ran into the difficulty of not having enough money for the considerable amount of lumber needed, this being very expensive in Mexico City because of the considerable construction then under way. In spite of this I gathered by donation here and there the wood needed to shore up the structure and build scaffolding until the Most Holy Virgin began to provide donations for buying beams for roofing, so that what was bought (which was the lesser part) and what was donated at the construction sites exceeded 100 pesos in value at the beginning. People marveled that in a time of such shortages so much wood was donated for the Nativitas monastery. Even though at the beginning I had to make do with one mason and two day laborers, God moved various masons and laborers from Mexico City who were attracted by the beauty of the Most Holy Virgin to go on foot and work for free on feast days. These work crews began with a boon that God granted to one Don Lorenzo Romero, who attributed the coincidence of circumstances to a miracle of Our Lady of Intercession and Our Father St. Francis. [P. 11, "March 1743" in margin.] This gentleman was the superintendent of a construction project. I went there and lamented to him the convent's imminent collapse if it was not reinforced. I asked him for some lumber. He granted me what he could, declaring that if the Most Holy Virgin and Our Father St. Francis supplied him with lime which, with the shortage, had risen in price to twenty-eight pesos a load, he would help me, and that I should send that Saturday or the following Monday for some beams. I promised him a mass, which I said that Saturday. On that day he went out looking for lime and could not find it even at twenty-eight pesos. But God showed him his beneficence on Monday: without even going out looking for lime, three loads arrived at eighteen pesos, the Divine Majesty repaying him one hundred percent, because for the beams he gave me he received double the lime, saving the considerable sum of thirty pesos. He was astonished and grateful. He ordered that I should be given whatever I asked for, and not only did he give me the first beams to begin reinforcing the monastery, he persuaded his many craftsmen to work for me for free. They brought others, and in this way God provided me with relief and even refreshment to give them by moving the spirit of *pulque*[11] producers to send me pulque with the boys who went to them for me, paying for their breakfast of tortillas and chiles. Indians of the pueblo transported the many beams I was able to obtain.

No. 13. [In margin: "March 1743"] In this transportation activity, the Devil caused them to become annoyed. When a general typhus epidemic struck the pueblo, in which about twenty Indian men and women fell victim, they excused themselves from carrying the wood, dismissing the dangers they could see with their eyes and becoming disheartened, saying that the rebuilding of the monastery which was underway did not need to be done, that only repairs here and there were needed. Having put this disinclination of the pueblo and other difficulties that presented themselves into the hands of the Most Holy Virgin, Our Father St. Francis, and St. Anthony with various masses that I said for this purpose, God moved their hearts with a manifest miracle that He put before their eyes. Twenty of the sick who had received extreme unction were almost in the throes of dying with various symptoms of typhus, without the aid of a physician or pharmacist, without food or clothing, their houses contaminated (because a few days before I had given the last rites to others in one of the houses). Seeing their resistance and wanting them to recognize that the construction was pleasing to God, I promised them in the name of God and his Most Holy Mother that none of the Indians who had received communion from me would die so that their small contributions to the construction would not be lost. To my astonishment and their encouragement, God chose to fulfill my promise. None of the adults died [p. 12], and they all got out of bed. Three children died, but I baptized thirteen. Seeing God's mercy, they changed greatly. Being so poor, so few, and without lands to plant or cultivate, I was encouraged by the wonders they were experiencing.

No. 14. Beginning of April 1743. In addition to the events I shall identify later, the Indians witnessed the times God rescued my person, undoubtedly through the intercession of his Most Holy Mother. One of them occurred when nineteen beams in the cloister, some broken at the head and others in the middle, were being reinforced. Having made a hole in the face of the wall to hold the head of a supporting beam that, once in place, would be secured at the other end, a mason was standing on a stepladder, holding the head of the supporting member so that it could be put in place. At the same time, another mason was on a flimsier ladder with a crowbar digging out the wall where it was to receive the breastwork, the ladder shaking as he struck with the tool. Another Indian was on the rung of another ladder, supporting the head of the breastwork, while another one was on the ground raising it with a length of wood, and another one was helping with a *matlacahuite*.[12] Seeing that the Indian day laborers were watching stupidly without offering help to support the base of the ladder so it would not slip when the mason struck with the crowbar, I scolded them, went under the ladder and, with both hands, drew it to my chest. Seeing me do this, a boy began to climb the ladder instead of staying below. As I was shouting to him not to climb up, the ladder I was holding in place broke apart and the Indian who was using the crowbar, the one who was supporting the breastwork, and the breastwork itself all fell straight toward me. I invoked the Most Holy Virgin as my head, brain, and spine were about to be struck by the force and weight of the breastwork. Somehow my body fell outside the wreckage, which fell across and extended full length in such an unlikely way that the ladder only struck one of my toes. Only the blow from falling to the ground hurt me a little on one side. Neither of those who fell from above landed on top of me, as would have been natural; nor were they injured. The crowbar remained stuck in the wall instead of falling with the man who was using it. The worker holding up the breastwork on the other side did not let go; he might have slipped off, but did not. I leave these circumstances for prudent reflection.

No. 15. At the end of April of the same year while putting on the amice to vest myself, I raised my eyes to the ceiling of the sacristy (because I was continually worried by the threat of its collapse). I saw four beams hanging loose in the center and did not want to vest myself under them. Later that afternoon I had the chest moved because I did not have the materials to reinforce them, [p. 13] having used up the materials I collected. After saying mass, I got on the mule and went to Don Joseph Pebedilla's house a quarter of a league[13] away. The embarrassment of asking specifically for four beams eight varas long bothered me, and I only asked him if, for the love of God, he would give me some beams to shore up the sacristy. He denied them to me in a cordial way, declaring that if the Most Holy Virgin got him out of a certain difficulty he had at hand, he would help me. I told him I would say a mass the next day to the Most Holy Queen so that he might be relieved of his concern. It grieved me inside that he had many beams in his yard, which I had seen, and was not moved to give me some that seemed to me to be about eight varas long. At that point I was taking my leave to come to Mexico City to look for beams. The conversation changed for a moment as I was saying goodbye and the Most Holy Virgin moved him to say, "Send for four beams, eight varas long." This left me astonished since he had not heard me say whether I wanted four and whether they needed to be eight varas long. Later I sent for them, and when the masons were removing the roof to put them in place the old beams fell without hurting anyone, some of them broken in the middle. They had not fallen in the preceding days despite the weight of the earthen covering and the trampling of the young Indians on the roof when they came to catechism class.

No. 16. The year 1743. On May 23, the day of Christ's Ascension, I decided to honor the Holy Sacrament and Our Lady and promote her cult by soliciting candle wax from my benefactors to celebrate Bermeo's jubilee[14] with the Holy Sacrament on view throughout the day. Having opened the sacrarium after the introit of the mass, I drew the cord of my Lady's curtain (I did not realize that she was exposed to view before I vested). In moving the rod, a large earthen jar of flowers filled with sand, which the sacristans had placed over the niche, came straight down over my head from a height of more than four varas. Judging by the location, it should have fallen directly on my head because I was standing behind the altar table, which was set back from the sacrarium more than a vara. The niche of the Most Holy Virgin was spared, as were the sacrarium and the candlesticks that were placed in front. My head was spared, too, for the jar fell behind me on the altar where it crashed to pieces and the sand scattered so that the whole altar table had to be cleaned. Here I pondered how I was saved from this jar (which should have fallen straight down) as it fell in an arc, landing about two varas from my head and the glass of the sacrarium door that covered the [p. 14] exceedingly beautiful image of Our Lord of the Ransom, a painting more than a vara in size that I left behind in 1740. In its fall the jar did not even threaten the four candlesticks of the sacrarium or the four others that were placed in front of the niche of my Lady; nor did a single candle break. All of this could not have happened without the intervention of a miracle.

No. 17. The year 1743. Having reroofed during March and April the greater part of seventeen varas of a corner covering three cells located over the *portería*,[15] the master builder of the city, Don Manuel Alvares, made ready to take up the floor of these cells and build a supplementary church there. I concurred, but without enthusiasm, to this start on the church, which was in no great danger of collapsing, while the convent needed immediate attention. I consulted Phelipe Alvares, brother of the master builder, and Dionicio Medina, master carpenter and very skilled in architecture, and the masons about dislodging the floor of the cells. They were very fearful that the entire span of cells would collapse and the project would cost many lives. In addition to the walls being swollen and uneven, the seventeen varas of the corner promised trouble and were half a vara out of line in the middle (both the inside walls and those of the portería). With this consultation, the Most Holy Virgin changed the plans of said Don Manuel Alvares and his brother who came most often to the project. He decided to demolish twenty varas of the corner because he recognized that the walls were out of line from carrying for so many years the weight of the thick, swollen material that had decomposed inside, supported only by the edges of the portería floor and cloister floors, dangling from side to side without other connection. He decided that even to take the roof down required extreme caution and that no beam should be removed from the middle of the span without removing those above so that they should not be without some substructure. Concerning these precautionary matters, after reasoned reflection I ordered that four progressively smaller braces be placed against the unsteady and leaning walls of the cloister. If the demolition had not been done many misfortunes would have resulted because removing the roof above the cells caused the beams to come loose in the middle, which was sagging the most (about half a vara) which in turn caused the span to open and fall directly on the cemetery in the corner of the portería; and if the corner of the cloister had not been braced it would have fallen on the convent. That all of these deliberations, resolutions, and actions were undertaken without loss of life to the masons, day laborers, those I paid on contract, and those who came periodically in crews to donate their labor, I attribute to miracles of the Sovereign Queen.

[p. 15]

No. 18. Faced with the urgency of starting to rebuild on the side where the portería is located, and needing much money to do so, I decided to bring the sovereign image to this city for a pilgrimage to many rich houses I knew and others I suspected, encouraged as I was by my confidence in the sponsorship of the Most Holy Virgin, who had provided so many donations to me for the Divine Cult during 1739 and 1740 and would not fail me now in my effort to rebuild the convent. Fearing the Indians' opposition because the Vicar General had ordered in 1740 when he went to bless the image that she not be removed from her niche, I came to confer with him about my plans. He applauded them heartily, saying that I should not be concerned about the Indians because he was disposed that I should encourage the faith and hope of such doubters who thought it was impossible for me to accomplish the rebuilding when I told them of my intentions to bring the Most Holy Image to Mexico City and showed themselves opposed and very resistant to letting me take the statue from its niche, much less from the pueblo. They appealed to the Vicar General in protest, but the result of this appeal was that he expressed his support for my plans and, reflecting on them carefully, he convinced the Indians with all seriousness that they should be grateful to me, and he ordered them to carry the Most Holy Image to this city. They did so and once I had accumulated 150 pesos in July and August, I returned the image to the pueblo in order to cheer them with its presence and for the celebration of their fiesta on September 8. On the fourteenth I arranged to return her to this city to provide me with the funds to work on her project.

No. 19. To this end I exhorted the pueblo to collect half a *real* for a votive mass to Our Lady which I would dedicate to the spiritual and temporal health of the entire pueblo and that of my benefactors as an act of thanks for the benefits received through the health that was completely restored to their sick members and for the good effect of my requests. I assured them that what was collected would be spent only on the construction. There was no difficulty with this proposal in comparison to the difficulty of getting them to give up the customary arrangement for paying clerical fees; nor was it difficult to persuade them to let the Most Holy Image return to this city. Having sung the mass, the salve, and litany with rogation, the Vicar General urged them to take heart and give up the shameful attitude implanted by the Devil about seeking donations for the temple and convent, and asked them what would be said about them in other pueblos? So we brought the Most Holy Image, and when I returned to the pueblo I found them so changed and eager to help me that they had already arranged by their own will to go on September 16 [p. 16] to the pueblo of Santa Martha four leagues away and ask for a donation of *tezontle*.[16] I had thought that there was no hope of acquiring this without a great deal of money, which we did not have. Who can doubt that this was a miracle of the Most Holy Virgin? It made me praise God to see the Indians going out as if they were certain of bringing back a great quantity, taking all of the little donkeys in the pueblo and mules that they could find. The Indian leaders were so committed to the endeavor that they asked me to order whippings for those who did not go to Santa Martha. Moved by this commotion, I went out at the same time to see Don Joseph

Pebedilla, who had given me the four eight-vara beams that I speak of
in paragraph number 15. On the road, as I was thinking about where I
could obtain hard rock to fill the foundations, I decided to pass by the
Augustinians' curacy of Ocoyoacac to ask the Reverend Father pastor
to help me. My journey to the said Pebedilla was to remind him of
the alms he owed for a mass that he asked me to sing to the Blessed
Sacrament, since I needed money to pay the skilled workers. But I
received all the help I hoped for without reminding him of the mass.
It happened that as soon as I entered his hacienda and fields I saw a
great deal of hard stone lying around. I coveted it for the foundations,
and after we exchanged greetings I asked him for that stone, if he did
not need it. He immediately gave to me, and much more from the
adjoining lands, saying to me in a serious tone, "There you have over
100 yards of hard stone, Father, and your Indians will not have to carry
as much as I can give you from the stony ground that is within the
lands of my hacienda. Send for it whenever you wish." Something else
happened then. While I was engaged in this conversation the Holy
Father Prior pastor of Ocoyoacac, who I wanted to go see, came to
visit. Learning of my ardent desire to undertake the construction, he
granted me as much help as he could for my project. One can imagine
how contented I was on the way home by so many marvels. I awaited
the Indians to tell them about it and find out what news they brought
about the tezontle. At the Angelus hour the poor little ones came in
very weighed down and tired, but very contented. They told me that
their request had been so well received by the pueblo of Santa Martha
that all of the Indian leaders had promised to make an additional
offering to the Most Holy Virgin of one yard of tezontle beyond the
great quantity they brought, on the condition that the Indians went
there for it. They said they would also give a great deal of tezontle and
teloyote.[17] Prudent reflection on the passages from paragraph number
17 to this point can only lead one to wonder at the repeated miracles
of Divine Providence and the sponsorship of the Sovereign Queen. To
all of this was added [p. 17] the business of the sand needed for the
mortar. The land of the pueblo being saline, *tequesquite,*[18] and clay, the
Indians discovered a great deposit of fine sand that the master builders
judged would make an excellent mortar.

No. 20. The year 1743. I continued my efforts in the capital, taking
this most beautiful image of the Sovereign Queen to many rich houses.
Being such a sacred lodestone of hearts, people would arrange a
special place for it and would not let me take it away for four or five
days, or sometimes nine days for a full novena. This was fine with
me because in the end they made generous donations in money or

precious jewels. Along the way, my Lady was covering the cost of the construction, demonstrating her sponsorship with frequent manifest miracles. The next miracle saved my life. It was witnessed by Doña Apolonia Garrote, wife of Don Manuel Ximenes de los Cobos (head of the postal service), and their entire family as they watched from above on the gallery of their house on Las Capuchinas Street. The said lady had asked me to bring her this Most Holy Image at the beginning of every month while it was in Mexico City in order to renew her devotion. Having brought it to her at the beginning of October 1743, I needed to take it to another house on the seventh. The Indians, having descended the stairs and raised the litter on their shoulders in the patio in order to leave, became terrified by a great commotion of kicking by eight mules that were tied up there, four to the pillars of the gallery and four to the iron rings of the front wall. In the crush the Indians could neither fall back nor turn around in order to reach the stairs because the mules' kicking left them no room. They would have to leave on their haunches to reach the clearing of the entryway. The risk that the kicks would reach the carriers and that the Most Holy Image would fall and break into pieces was obvious. God willed that no kick reached the Indians even though barely three-quarters of a vara on each side separated them from the haunches of the mules. I went along the side with the pillars where one mule was kicking most strenuously (excited, I believed, by the Devil). He launched four kicks at my head and my only protection was to move my head toward my Lady's pedestal, urgently invoking her protection so that the mule's kicks would not kill me. I swear in verbo sacerdotis that, to the astonishment of the lady and her family who were watching from above, the mule's iron shoes resonated next to my ear about an inch away [p. 18] and on my cheek and right temple I felt the air move from the mule's hooves. If I had not protected myself by turning to the left and putting my head on the Most Holy Virgin's pedestal, invoking her protection, I would have been killed on the spot. This was a miracle of the Sovereign Queen. And it was also a miracle that when one of the Indians in front of me let go of the litter, the others did not let go. Here I do not remember if I counterbalanced the litter with my left shoulder until we escaped that danger by reaching the entryway.

No. 21. The year 1743. In this same house at the beginning of November when I took the Holy Image again to Doña Apolonia, the Sovereign Queen performed another miracle because the hearts of that entire family had remained so touched, even more fervently, since the previous month when they were witnesses to the manifest danger to my life among the hooves of the mule that was kicking at me. A maid of theirs named María was dangerously ill from an extremely grave obstruction or abscess formed around the great quantity of chalk she had eaten as a girl. This abscess passed to her stomach and formed a great ball. Finding herself without a remedy, even with those that the most reputable physicians prescribed, she put all her hopes in the Sovereign Queen, the source of health for the sick, having faith that with her Holy Image in the house, she would make her well. With this hope she drank a home remedy in the Virgin's name and began to expel that stone through her urinary track. One infers that the stone, which must have been large, now dissolved into small fragments, some the size of chickpeas, others smaller; some white, others yellow or black; and many grains. In the act of expelling them the roughness of the large pieces and the ones that were as sharp as flints caused fainting spells, discharges of blood, and mortal agony. Any of the fragments could have consumed her, but with the aid of Our Lady, to whom she promised to take communion in her honor and visit her in her temple as soon as I returned the image to the pueblo, she completely recovered her health and was relieved of the abscess. I learned of all of this from the said Doña Apolonia who told me every word of it and showed me the maid [p. 19] safe and sound. She showed me many stones and told me that the royal physician Don Joseph Valentín had taken away some others. I asked her for some of them to send to the temple at the right time along with a devotional painting sponsored by Doña Apolonia so that the miracle could be publicized. And I asked her to give me in a little glass container a quantity of the small stones so that they could be placed in the niche. The said lady swore to me that the number of these little stones expelled by the maid would fill a plate. She gave me a little glass container filled with them so that they could be placed in the niche of Our Lady at the appropriate time after the miracle was authenticated. The authentication never took place because I was removed from the convent and my pastoral assignment came to an end, but to this day I keep the little stones in a piece of paper on which I wrote about this miracle in a few sentences.

No. 22. Since I began the construction of the convent I commended my efforts to the prayers of the nuns of the convents where I was a confessor and to other prayers of other worthy souls. For this reason I shall not leave out what happened to me during that same month of November when I was suffering a great affliction because the lime was used up, I had no money to pay the people, and I owed seventy pesos toward the one hundred pesos I had borrowed from Don Domingo Laureano de la Vega, master pharmacist and my intimate friend from

Santa Inés Street who himself borrowed them in order to make me
the loan. Shortly after carrying the Most Holy Virgin to his house, a
pious Dominican nun dressed in the habit of St. Rose happened by to
venerate the Holy Image (she was one of my spiritual daughters and
of a very pure soul). As soon as I saw her, I said in jest, "Pious sister,
I won't ask you for silver or gold, only an hour of fervent prayers to
God to give me many pesos to build a church and convent to this most
miraculous image. See how afflicted I am today!" She replied, "Well,
my father, Your Reverence should have a novena prayed to
St. Cajetan. I will start it today very devoutly and I know that he will
help you." The next day I went to the house of the Syndic General,
Don Miguel de Hortigosa, who looked kindly upon me for I had
already taken the Most Holy Image of Our Lady to his house. After
a good conversation on this occasion (no doubt advanced by the
Sovereign Lady) he ordered his cashiers to count out 200 pesos for me.
Seeing such a timely donation and thanking him heartily, I told him
of the extreme need in which I found myself and urged him to tell me
which benefactor had put that [p. 20] donation in his hands. He told
me to take the money for my project and ask no more questions. Here
I inferred that Our Very Reverend Father Navarrete had visited the
house (since they were intimate *compadres*[19] and fellow countrymen),
had grasped the beauty of the Most Holy Image on one of the
occasions I had left it there and, satisfied by my efforts, would have
ordered the said Syndic to give me that donation without telling me
who the donor was. But who cannot worship the providence of God
and the sponsorship of his Most Holy Mother in relieving my urgent
need, giving me the funds to buy a good deal of lime, pay my people,
and have seventy pesos left to turn over to Don Domingo de la Vega?
God chose to fulfill a proposal Don Domingo had made me two weeks
before when I had brought fifty pesos and then another twenty toward
the 100 pesos he had lent me, repaying them before the date promised.
At that time he said, "I do not accept this money as payment but I shall
keep it for Your Reverence in this purse for when you may need it."
And the day the Syndic gave me the 200 pesos I told Don Domingo,
"Today God wishes to confirm that you are keeping seventy pesos for
me. Here you see the 100 pesos I owe you, and another 100 pesos that
God has given me I shall take to buy lime and pay my people; and
the seventy pesos you are keeping for me I won't take to the Syndic
because Friday I need to buy another three loads of lime." God willed
that during that month of great affliction in November, even though
my expenses were more than 440 pesos, I took in almost 350 pesos,
the most I have had in a month since the construction began. In this

the Sovereign Queen undoubtedly made her presence felt, repeatedly working miracles.

No. 23. The year 1743. Having taken her Most Holy Image to the house of Dr. Buitrón, his niece Doña Manuela prayed to the Virgin most devoutly, making her many supplications that from that day forward gambling should cease in a certain house, which had caused great disquiet to her conscience. She asked for it with such force and so many pleas to Our Lady that it was granted to her, and from that day forward no one gambled in that house again, so she told me. And being pregnant and fearing that something bad would happen during the delivery, she affirmed to me that she attributed the uncomplicated birth to the sponsorship of Our Lady, to whom she had entrusted herself.

No. 24. The year 1743. In the house of Dr. Don Joseph Pinal, his sister, to whom I had taken the Most Holy Image, told me that she had appealed to Our Lady with much insistence for the prompt completion of a certain matter that was very important to her, saying to her with devout daring and in a formal way, "Look, my soul, now that you are revealing yourself in your most beautiful image of the Intercession, by this title please do me the favor of this and this. Since this is the first boon I have requested of you under this advocation, I am certain that my trust will not be misplaced." She told me that the Most Holy Virgin granted her wishes just as she requested. I record it for her glory [p. 21].

No. 25. During November, in consideration of the Most Holy Virgin's repeated miracles through her most beautiful image and having taken her on pilgrimage to so many houses, I came to the conclusion that it would be better (I should say that the Sovereign Queen was responsible) for my unworthiness and meagerness to make the advocation of her Intercession known and worshiped in a most solemn Rosary procession. The first thing I decided to do was find a benefactor who would pay for her portrait on a polished copper plate so that three or four thousand prints could be made. Very soon Don Francisco Unzueta, master gold wire drawer in Monterilla Street, agreed to sponsor it, and the engraving of the copper plate was done. The excellent Troncoso who did the work (and who took the original home with him) was advised to leave a space on the plate at the foot of the Holy Image for six or seven lines because my second project had to do with remembering fondly the notable favors I owed to the Most Illustrious, Most Excellent Señor Vizarrón (which I noted on pages 7–8 of paragraph number 8). He recognized in my report about the deplorable state of the convent and church, the manifest miracles and marvels that were happening, and the need to support the rebuilding by the pilgrimage of the Most Holy Image in this capital as a way to collect donations. Now I was asking His Most Illustrious Excellency for permission to publicize the devotion and donations by making the devotion known in a solemn Rosary and asking him to grant the indulgences he deemed appropriate. I obtained it all by his decree, which is documented later on, which I presented, as required, to the Vicar General for confirmation of the license for the Rosary.

No. 26. Having obtained both decrees on the same day, December 2, 1743, it was all a mad rush because the substance of the Archbishop's decree needed to be engraved on the plate and a suitable event for the distribution of the prints was still to be arranged. All of this was done with the money provided me by Divine Providence. And since I was blessed by God since my youth with a not unrefined poetic muse in Spanish and Latin, in all meters, I composed the sonnet that appears below, although my poor mental faculties were absorbed at the time in the many diverse affairs that blocked my way, including the construction, the present commitment which gave me no peace, my ardent desire to go to the pueblo and return to Mexico City with Indians to carry the Holy Image because, with the frequent miracles that were occurring, it was being requested in various homes and I did not dare trust it to the Indian carriers of Mexico City because those from the pueblo were already trained in how to mount the pedestal on the platform and undo it in order to carry it up the stairs of the homes without smudging the detailing in gold leaf on this most beautiful image.

No. 27. With the sonnet printed in a rush, in four days I arranged for December 6–8 for the public devotion by all the residents of the Salto del Agua neighborhood and the guards of the city gate, who were especially devoted to the Most Holy Image. In order to spread the approbation, they arranged—beginning on the second when I told them of the Archbishop's decree and the printing—for many gatherings, a procession, and a very brilliant and dignified masked ball on the seventh, and a triumphal carriage in which they displayed the Holy Image of the Immaculate Conception that is venerated at the Salto del Agua chapel. At three o'clock the assorted parties that I gave by the hundreds left from the city gate acclaiming Most Holy Mary throughout the city in an exemplary way (as I cautioned them to do) along the route that the [p. 22] Rosary was to follow. The morning of the seventh they asked me to permit a number of parties in all the corners and doorways of the churches. And since I had taken this Most Holy Image to the houses of the dean and canons, I obtained from the dean the very notable, unprecedented favor that once the matins had been prayed and even if the sun had gone down, I would be allowed to bring the Rosary procession into the cathedral by the first door of Forgiveness, make the accustomed circuit, and leave by the third door. This was done, and from there the procession went down Seminario Street, turned at the church of St. Theresa, and passed the Archbishop's palace, where the archbishop prostrated himself before the Most Holy Virgin. From there it went to the palace residence, then to San Joseph de Gracia and the church of Regina Coeli. The entire city was deeply affected by this Rosary. The streets were in glory because, in addition to the balconies and windows being adorned with hangings, melodies resounded from various musical groups that spontaneously joined in order to go along singing impressively; and at intervals the first half of the Ave Maria was said and the entire gathering gave the response. I went in front with a stole over my robes, intoning the mysteries of the crown. And because the dean told me that he had ordered the sacristans not to close the cathedral doors until the Rosary passed, they were waiting until just before dusk when the matins were completed. Meanwhile the procession left Santa Clara where Our Lady was being kept, turned at Vergara Street to go along Plateros, and from there to the cathedral. And since it was almost dusk by then and the days were so short, all the streets were alight with lanterns, even the government offices, and the great houses had lighted braziers[20] on their balconies and fired off salvos of rockets. Crowds of people gathered on both sides of the streets and far to the rear where they were following Our Lady. And in addition to the many lanterns that were brought, many people were supplied with wax candles, many of which I paid for. At eight o'clock in the evening the Rosary entered the Regina church with a litany. Once that was finished, I intoned the hymn in honor of the Eucharist, the great crowd responding with the choir. I took my leave, calling out my many thanks. The cost of this Rosary exceeded 200 pesos. God provided it all, and his Most Holy Mother obtained it, as I will describe in the right place on the leaf following the exceedingly beautiful engraving of Our Lady of Intercession and the sonnet with which my ardent desire caused such solemnity. Further on I will recount the last miracle of those that Our Lady did in 1743 in this same Regina Coeli church after her Holy Rosary was over.

[p. 23]

[Attached to the reverse side of this print is a printed page with the two poems by de la Rosa, one formed in an acrostic, the other eight lines long. This page also repeats the indulgence granted by the Archbishop, and ends with an appeal for the display of lanterns, torches, and rockets as the Rosary procession passes.]

Print from the copper-plate engraving of Our Lady of the Intercession that de la Rosa commissioned. Courtesy of the Biblioteca Nacional de México, Fondo Reservado.

Siempre, ó Mexico, siempre ...... De MA........ RIA
Aplaude Grac.... las, sol... Eterniza Glo.... ias,
Dedica Te....... Xplos cu....... rtos, y mem... orias
La tu .... Amante c....... Ath............ lica hidalguia
Tero s........... Siempre en tu a. Xparo e........ noche, y dia,
A circulos........ Xilagros....... à victoria....
Toda........... Armas, toda..... Luces, tod...... Glorias
Reyna, ¶ Abo.... Cada, M....... Adre, Estrell ... y Guia
Cy pu........... Ms qual Pere... Crina sin Santua... io
Convento,....... Zi Alcaza .... R su G...... andeza
Injuriosos....... Del tiemp..... O à los r....... gores
Zoticias qui ...... Pre darte en... Su Rosar ..... o
Ten............. Zuevas marav... Ullas que ...... y su Alteza
Obr.......... P en su........ Esta. Imagen à fav Cres

Qui elucidant me vitam aternam ha-   *Facite vobis sacculos qui non veterascunt the-*
bebunt. Eccli. cap. 24. ÿ. 31.   *saurumnon deficienté in Cælis. Luc. c. 11.*

(La que es de la gracia abysmo,)   (Y el Seraphin su devoto,   )
(Te insinùa en este Rosario,   )   (Llagado esta obra te acuerda,)
(Mexico, que en su Santuario   )   (Y afianza en su Saco, y Cuerda,)
(Hagas bien para ti mismo.   )   (No la eches en saco roto.   )

El Ilmo. y Excmo. Señor Doctor Don Juan Antonio de Vizar-
ron, y Eguiarreta, Arzobispo de Mexico, por su Decreto de 2.
de Diciembre del año de 1743. concede quarenta dias de Indul-
gencia à todas, y â cada una de las personas de uno, y otro sexo,
que pidiendo à Dios devotamente por el feliz estado de la mili-
tante Iglesia, exaltacion de nuestra Santa Fè Catholica, concur-
rieren con su limosna para la fabrica material del arruinado Tem-
plo, y Convento nombrado Nra. Sra. de Nativitas, extra-muros
de dicha Ciudad, como tambien à todas las que no pudiendo
dar limosna rezaren tres Ave Marias ante la milagrosissima Imagen de Nra. Sra. del Patrocinio de dicho Convento, por los
que la dieren para el mencionado reedificio

Se pide por amor de Dios Salva de luminarias, faroles, y cohetes, ma-
ñana à las nueve de la noche, y todo el dia miercoles colgaduras en
las ventanas, para las tres de la tarde que passará el Rosario
en el qual se suplica devoto acompañamiento.
de ura los que pudieren

De la Rosa's poems for the Rosary procession. Courtesy of the Biblioteca Nacional
de México, Fondo Reservado.

[p. 24]

No. 28. The year 1743. Margarita de Villavicencio, the unmarried mulatto daughter of Francisco Villavicencio and Sebastiana de Amaya, had been suffering for two years from a most grave abscess in among her liver, kidneys, and stomach, the result of a serious blow or fall, for which she had not taken medicine soon enough. The night of December 8, 1743, as the Rosary procession of the Most Holy Queen of Heaven was passing her house she joined in on the way to the church of Regina Coeli shouting her supplications for recovery to the Virgin because all the physicians and surgeons of Mexico City had given up hope. Bleeding from the mouth and expelling pus during the previous eight months, she had been unable to walk or sleep because of the continual fever. She seemed sentenced to fall down dead at any moment. But her faith and confidence in She who brings health to the sick was cheered and she followed the Most Holy Image, almost dragging herself along, pleading to the image where it was placed behind the altar inside the church. Even when the others had left, she stayed by the altar, incessantly imploring until eight o'clock at night when the nuns, at my request, were waiting in the entry to take the Most Holy Image inside the convent. The marvel is that from that hour on this sick woman felt no more pains, returning home without them. The next day she expelled the abscess in her bowel movements and became well. The surgeon Arlazón who examined her and had many times before given up all hope was astonished by her sudden return to health and judged it a miracle. Not only did he stand ready to swear it, he also encouraged other physicians to do so who many times had despaired of her recovery. I was unaware of this most manifest miracle until several months later. Although I knew at the time that a woman was imploring Our Lady behind the altar, I did not take any interest except to protect the jewels that the Most Holy Image was wearing, which were worth more than three hundred pesos, by having the nuns take it into the convent and place in the lower choir. The occasion for me to learn about this most manifest miracle had to do with the Most Holy Virgin: I was taking the Most Holy Image to another house several months into the next year and as I passed this woman's house she rushed out devoutly elated, exclaiming in the street her fervent thanks to Our Lady, recounting this miracle publicly just as I have written it. I swear to it in verbo sacerdotis; and [p. 25] to record the account in detail I am certain that I took the Most Holy Image into this woman's house (although I do not remember the address) and asked for an inkwell and pen, which were found, and took down all the details and the woman's name and her parents' names in order to transfer them exactly to my notebook. From those notes I have made this clean and better-organized version of the history and the marvels I experienced from the Most Holy Virgin by means of her Most Holy Image. And having recorded the miracles of 1743 to this point, I shall continue with those that took place during the rest of the year.

No. 29. The year 1743. Miracle with the print. That same day of the Immaculate Conception of Our Lady and her solemn Rosary, Xaviera de N., wife of Casimiro the Marqués de Guardiola's coachman, experienced the protection of the Sovereign Queen. Being pregnant and suffering from a grave swelling in the face, she wanted them to extract a molar. As a result of this absurdity her gums became infected, from which she expelled basins full of pus and experienced extreme pain in the vast swelling while still in bed from only recently having given birth. Hearing of the miracles of Our Lady of Intercession, she fervently asked for a print from the engraving; and applying it to herself with great feeling and devotion the pains she was suffering immediately ceased. She slept through the night and those that followed after not being able to sleep for two months. The next day she expelled four fetid little bones, which would be the roots of her tooth, and became well again.

No. 30. The year 1743. At the end of December I took the Most Holy Image to the house of the master builder Don Joseph Gonzales who freely gave of his skill and helped me with the construction. Upon entering with my Lady, Don Joseph's mother, Doña Catharina, said to her in my presence, "Lady of my heart, even though I have been suffering this *mal de madre*[21] for twenty years, I shall continue to offer you your incense, candles, and fragrances. You know whether I shall be freed from this illness, but I have confidence in you, that you are going to cure me." And a marvelous thing happened! From that very hour, I gather, the twenty years of fainting ended. The poison of this illness (which are the vapors) turned into an antidote, for the mal de madre never returned.

No. 31. The year 1743. In the same month of December Juan Leonardo, unmarried Indian of the pueblo who worked as a salaried laborer on the construction, was climbing a scaffold with a load of stone. The rope holding the scaffold together came undone or broke and he fell to the ground from a distance of more than six varas, invoking Our Lady on the way down. He fell on a heap of stones, and a beam from the scaffold fell on top of him. This might well have killed him, and only the Sovereign Queen could have saved him. In a few days he recovered from the injury to his foot and the bruises to his body, and was well enough to continue working [p. 26].

MIRACLES OF OUR LADY IN THE YEAR 1744

No. 32. The year 1744. On January 20, I was taking the Most Holy Image from the house of Don Phelipe Narvarte to the Hospital de Jesús Nazareno and residence of Royal Physician Torres. Upon turning the corner for the hospital we were extremely terrified, as was everyone on the street, by a horrible thunderclap as if from an unexpected bolt of lightning. A hundred pounds of gunpowder had unexpectedly exploded in the fireworks factory on the royal street of the slaughterhouse below the hospital bridge and right in front of Don Joseph de Urizar's house. In the havoc and clamor of the blast the doors of the fireworks factory were blown to bits. This fright did not make me retreat; rather, near the chapel of Santa Iphigenia I arranged for my Lady to enter the portico of the hospital. Although my confidence in her protection and the manifest miracles that were being experienced convinced me to carry her to where the fire was engulfing the factory, I did not resolve to do so, fearful that the crowd of people and palace guards who had arrived would trample the Indians and the Most Holy Image would be broken to pieces. But at the urging of my companion, the lay brother Fray Agustín Zuleta, my Lady was brought out and he went in front with me, asking for room to pass, and the gathering of people made room with great veneration so she could be taken to the portico of Don Joseph de Urizar's house, which was a stone's throw from the fire. At that moment a horrible cloud of smoke came from the burning factory and greatly endangered the residence that was above the factory because the upper timbers were already aflame. But no sooner had the sovereign image arrived and the gathering clamored for her protection than the fire went out and the danger ceased faster than it would take to pray a Credo. All those present were astonished and acclaimed the event, shouting "Miracle, miracle of Our Lady of Intercession." The Most Holy Queen continued to make her presence felt for, once the fire was extinguished and the danger had passed, as I was bringing her to the hospital, she brought with her a mulatto who was wounded all over his body and being carried on a plank. I say that she brought him with her to the hospital, under her protection, because only Spaniards were admitted there, yet his being a mulatto was no obstacle in this case because of the respect owed to Most Holy Mary who had just performed a miracle by extinguishing the fire. How could the Sovereign Queen fail to help this mulatto who every week gave half a real[22] to Fray Agustín Zuleta for the convent's building fund? Here this friar marveled at the profound judgments of God, as did I: he reported to me that three days before, when he had gone to the fireworks factory to ask for donations for Our Lady, one of the workers rudely said to him, "I'll make no donation, father," and the mulatto responded, "but I will do it, Father," and took out his half real. Fray Agustín marveled that Our Lady protected the mulatto but not the other man, whose head was broken by a plank in the devastation done by the fire [p. 27].

No. 33. The year 1744. The day after the miracle of the extinguished fire I took this Most Holy Image from the hospital because Licenciado Don Manuel Nolasco, ordained priest and attorney of the Tribunal of the Santa Cruzada, asked me to have her visit an eight-year-old girl named María Nicolasa, daughter of Don Balthasar Sánchez and Doña Mariana Molina, who was in mortal danger from a nasty case of typhus with very dangerous symptoms. She was already in the death throes when the Most Holy Image of Our Lady was brought in. And once she arrived the patient's agony abated in an evident and sudden recovery (which I witnessed). Undoubtedly the mother's keen faith and resignation were responsible, plus a steady confidence in which I exhorted her. I told her that she should take it for a certainty that once Our Lady was present (because at that point she had not yet entered the house) the child would either worsen and die or begin to recover; that whether she chose for her to die or live would be quickly known, and that she should dedicate herself to Our Lady whether the child lived or not, promising her that if the girl lived she would make her the Virgin's special devotee, dressing her in a little habit and spreading the news of the miracle. She promised Our Lady to do so, and as soon as her Holy Image was brought to where the child was about to die and one of the prints was applied to her, she came to and began to recover. Five days later when I returned to the house to take my Lady, I found the child crying because she wanted to eat a big meal and stop drinking broth.

No. 34. The year 1744, with the print. At the end of January, the same Licenciado Don Manuel Nolasco bore witness to me that Ana María de N., wife of the barber Antonio de N. and spiritual daughter of said gentleman, was about to succumb to a great pain in her side. Her husband went to inform this gentleman that the patient was in the throes of death and they were helping her to have a good death and entrust herself to God. Hearing this he gave the husband his print of Our Lady, telling him that he feared he was about to lose her, but that he should go quickly and apply it to the patient's side with great faith. And as soon as he applied it, the paroxysm ceased and the patient began to recover from the mortal danger. This esteemed priest, whom I knew and had dealings with over many years as a very wise and sensible man, told me this with astonishment.

No. 35. The year 1744. In this month of January an unmarried Indian of the pueblo named Agustín Roxas, son of the widower Diego de Santiago, was working as a mason's helper on the construction of the convent. A coach was stuck in the mire in front of the site and he wanted to help pull it out on the side that was leaning. As they were lifting it, the mules pulled violently and he was caught underneath. As the wheels passed over his thigh, stomach, chest, and shoulder he invoked the Most Holy Virgin with all his heart and he was freed miraculously from the wheel passing over his head. It is astonishing that he did not succumb from the wheels passing across his stomach and chest when he invoked Our Lady. Although his bones were dislocated from this accident and he was confined to bed in a bad state, it was God's will that, without the aid of a physician or pharmacist, he recovered and continued to work on the construction. I witnessed this and he told me about the miracle.

[p. 28]

No. 36. The year 1744, miracle with the print. Pedro Días a *castizo*[23] carder from the Barrio de Santa María and his wife had a five-year-old son named Anacleto whose head had been rotting since birth. A great deal of stench and matter and some little bones oozed from his ears. As a result he was deaf and also so mute that in his pain he could only explain himself by signs. When his parents heard about the miracles that Our Lady was working through her Most Holy Image of the Intercession, they welcomed her and frequently touched their son with one of the prints, promising her a pound of wax with which to keep vigil and to take their child to the temple as soon as she returned there. At the beginning of February they continued to implore the Sovereign Queen with these promises, begging for the recovery of their son so that he could hear and speak. A wondrous thing happened, for while they were repeating these promises the child suddenly began to articulate words that, because of deafness, he had never heard, and he pronounced them as if he had heard them and learned them. Losing this muteness was an astonishing marvel, and recovering from the infection in his head was another. In the barrio of Santa María the father was known as Pedro the carder. He was my compadre and esteemed me highly because when I was the pastor of Santa María I baptized a son of his in 1742 in the Veracruz parish. In February 1744 he told me about this prodigious event as I have written it here. I swear it in verbo sacerdotis.

No. 37. The year 1744. On February 5 when we were taking the Most Holy Image of Our Lady past the house of Josepha Ocaysola, who was suffering from severe pain to her head and face, she came out to prostrate herself. She said, "Lady, take away this pain and I promise to bring you a peso for a mass or for your building even though you know that right now I do not have even half a real." At that instant the pain that had so afflicted her disappeared. The master builder Don Joseph Gonsales, who supervised the construction and knew the woman, told me about this.

No. 38. The year 1744, miracle with the print. On March 2 Don Joseph Zequeira, former page of the Most Illustrious and Esteemed Elizacochea, Bishop of Guadiana, and resident of this capital, fell mortally ill from a furious typhus, pain in his side, pneumonia, and affliction in his chest. The illness was running its course with mortal nausea and he was prepared to die. Meanwhile three reputable physicians who visited him and gave up hope were dismissed because their medicines did him no good. While almost in the throes of death, although still alert, he was shown the Most Holy Image of Our Lady in the form of a print that had been brought to him at the beginning of the illness. Already succumbing, he seemed to see the Holy Image in a vivid likeness and, not being able to speak, he made a vow in his heart to go and personally serve on the construction of her convent or to labor on the project, even if it was only to carry a crate, if he were given a lay brother's habit (since he was too old to be an aspirant to the priesthood) [p. 29]. As soon as he made this interior vow he obtained such relief that the next day he sat up to feed himself, which he had not been able to do without assistance since falling ill; and the following day he dressed himself, to the surprise of those who knew of his grave condition, especially Doña María Ortiz, lay member of the Third Order of Our Father St. Francis, who was helping him and who lived opposite "Christ's chain." She told me of these events and ordered a painting in memory of this miracle of Our Lady. She is ready to swear it at any time, and she can name others who will swear to it, as well. As I was redoing the accounts of these prodigious events this year of 1775, I recalled that around 1754 when I was living in this monastery in Mexico City (where I have been living for thirty years), this good gentleman was living as a lay brother in the infirmary, fulfilling his vow since 1745 when I came to live in this monastery, when Our Father Provincial Arratia granted him the habit. I spoke to him many times, and he would recall with deep gratitude this miracle of the Sovereign Queen.

No. 39. The year 1744, miracle with the print. In March during the second week of Lent my great friend Don Domingo de la Vega (who I mention in paragraph number 22) fell mortally ill. The complications confounded this knowledgeable and excellent pharmacist and the most skillful physicians. A bleeding or purging was indicated, but he could not be bled or purged because if the lightest purging was done or a drop of blood taken, even if it was done with a leech, his body twitched and he would faint. He was given the last rites and was in the throes of death in between mortal fainting spells. On top of this, when he stood up or walked or mounted a horse or coach, or caught the slightest cold or did a bit of writing, he was beset by a mortal fever. He was exceptionally devoted to this most miraculous image of Our Lady, which I twice took to his house. Confident of her protection, he resolved to follow the physicians' instructions and, embracing one of the prints he placed it on his brain and prepared for the application of a single leech. It had barely begun to extract blood when, in a mortal fainting spell he was attacked with a convulsion in his right hand and leg; but it did not reach his brain and head where he had placed the print because Our Lady wished it known that his escape from death on that occasion must have been by a miracle. The convulsions and fainting spells continued and the physicians despaired for his life (even though they had the most exquisite remedies at hand). They ordered that he be given extreme unction and helped to achieve a good death. Seeing this, I took my Lady from the house of another benefactor, brought it to the sick man, and placed it [p. 30] near the bed. They thought he was going to expire, but he experienced the protection of the Sovereign Queen because, even though the fainting spells continued (for which reason I stayed in the house that night helping him and keeping vigil), he recovered and the danger passed. He pondered the fact that from the time the print was placed on his brain for the operation with the leech the convulsion did not reach his brain; and he was even more encouraged by the presence in his house of the original miraculous image. He declared that he owed his life to Most Holy Mary. After he recovered and was able to get up, it amazed me that he could exercise strenuously for several days in his delicate state and not feel worse than he used to feel from the slightest exertion.

No. 40. The year 1744, miracle with the print. On May 24, the Sunday of the Holy Spirit, María Tamariz, a creole[24] married to Joseph de Lara who lived at the Puente del Fierro in houses known as de la Colegiala, successfully gave birth. But that evening for some unknown reason she was overcome by a most uncontrollable rage. By six o'clock they judged her to be raving mad, to the point that she wanted to throw the infant over the screen. They kept watch over her during the night so she would not kill the infant and because they realized that she could not sleep. The physician said she was mad and that they might have to prevent her from suffocating her child or going out into the open air undressed and endangering herself with more illness. In this predicament Doña María Gertrudis Romero, who knew of the miracles of Our Lady of Intercession, devoutly placed one of the prints upon her, telling her to entrust herself to the original image whose miracles were so renowned throughout this city. Hearing this, she exclaimed to Our Lady in wholehearted agreement and immediately her fury subsided and she said she wanted to sleep. At this point Don Diego de Paz, son of the said Doña María Romero and master silversmith, had brought to his house the crown of Our Lady to solder a piece of it (which was broken in the house where I had taken it). Taking advantage of this circumstance, the said Doña María decided to take it to the sick woman, who pleaded that it be placed on her pillow, repeatedly saying to Our Lady that she wanted to sleep. She slept all that night and the following day until the crown was taken to the house where the Most Holy Image was. The image was brought to her and, now very much in possession of her faculties, she repeated her request to the Virgin for sleep. She did sleep and was left cured of the madness. Doña María Gertrudis told me all that I set down here as a witness to the events and participant in bringing the crown of Our Lady to the sick woman [p. 31].

No. 41. The year 1744, miracle with the print. All the people of the pueblo who were living in 1744 and are still alive can attest to the following miracle as well as I can in verbo sacerdotis. On Saturday August 8, I was called to confess Dominga María, wife of Bernardo Antonio, who, a few days short of giving birth, fell on her stomach while jumping over a little ditch and killed the child. From that point on she felt no movement, only extreme pain, which she endured with imprudent silence. Finally, overwhelmed by the pain, she went into labor. By the sixth day only a little hand of the dead child had emerged. That morning they called on me, telling me about all of this. Considering the danger because I could smell her stinking breath and knew the carelessness of the Indians because of their negligence and poverty, I told her that in that delicate situation the best she could do was appeal to the Most Holy Virgin for a miracle and entrust herself to her protection with great faith and promise her some communions, rosaries, or attendance at masses, and become her devotee. I urged her relatives to come to Mexico City for a surgeon to twist out the corpse. They brought him and he began to remove the corpse by parts. It was so decayed that they told me it was necessary to break it into pieces, which sounded like ribbed silk coming out. The body became stuck on the lower jawbone so that the head, neck, and placenta remained inside. So as not to martyr her further and consume her in the process, the surgeon left her in that condition to see if she would expel it naturally. But this did not happen even with potions provided free of charge by the famous Don Vicente Rebeque. Still in great pain, she asked for extreme unction, and I brought it to her with the greatest compassion. Having made her vow of faith, I gave her one of the prints of my Lady, exhorting her to apply it to her stomach with intense faith once she had received the sacrament and oil. In taking my leave with the Eucharist, I had them help her lie down in order to bless her with the Sacrificed Lord. I knelt, placed the sacred vessel over her head, and prayed two prayers to the Most Holy Virgin. Then I left; but before I reached the church the head and placenta, green with putrefaction, came out and she began to improve. And so she continued for two days, quite a sign of her miraculous liberation from such a grave danger. Her recovery would have continued if the ignorant Indian women had not made her drink what was left of Rebeque's potion for her to expel the infant. They thought it was a purgative, but it brought on bloody dysentery, which killed her.

No. 42. The year 1744. During June, Don Joseph Gonsales, master architect who lent his services to the construction project without charging, commiserated with me about the many tribulations he was enduring with his wife. We discussed whether the many excesses observed in her behavior were madness. They seemed more to be obsessions or possessions by an evil spirit than madness because, without speaking, she did not harm anyone but herself as she put her life in manifest danger. Formerly a playful and talkative woman [p. 32] (although very chaste and judicious), she had gone nearly mute. When asked "Woman, who makes you do what you do?" she would answer only "the youngsters." I began to wonder whether she was possessed by demons because she would chew pieces of China plates and would eat them as if they were sweet cakes, with manifest danger of shredding her gullet and intestines. And she would sit next to a wall, her thighs and legs drawn up to her chest, and begin to scrape the wall with her fingernails; making a hole in the wall, she would eat the masonry and build a little vault with the stones she separated out and put everything inside it. She went out to the stable and without anyone's help gave birth. God disposed that they would go looking for her and discover an evident marvel: the infant girl having come out, somehow she did not suffocate even though her neck was constricted by the umbilical cord. Undoubtedly the infant's guardian angel had protected her for she had put her little hands between the cord and her neck, stretching the cord enough to breathe and not expire without baptism. She was, in fact, baptized, and through it all, the mother was

as fresh as if nothing had happened to her, blaming "the youngsters."
When I heard this I thought that there were demons involved and
I resolved that we should take her to Bachelor Don Joseph Castro,
sacristan of the Hospital del Amor de Dios, whom the Divine Majesty
had granted special ability to exorcise demons and discover diabolical
spells. He exercised this power under license from the Inquisition.
Many people went to him, as I can attest. I promised Don Joseph
Gonsales to go see this blessed priest so that his wife could be taken
to him to see if there were some signs of possession by the Devil or
a spell. An Indian carrier brought her (they are accustomed to carry
women) and she put up no resistance even in the presence of Father
Castro and various people who were seated on the floor up against
the wall. She did not react at all; nor did she speak a word; nor did the
others who were there waiting for the priest to exorcise them react in
any way. Seeing this, I had the Indian carry her out, resolving in my
mind to exorcise her in the pueblo church before the Most Holy Image
of Our Lady as soon as she was brought back to the church. Once the
image was returned in July, and seeing the poor husband so afflicted
and fearful of his wife's absurdities because she was in the last months
of pregnancy, I told him to bring her. In order to exorcise her with the
special incantation contained in the *flagellum Demonis*,[25] I deceived
the Indians about the proceedings by telling them that because our
benefactor the master builder [p. 33] and his wife were expecting a
child and the wife's life was in danger from an illness, I had decided
to have her brought in order to be blessed in front of the Eucharist
and the miraculous image of Our Lady. The husband brought her (I
do not recall if she came in a sedan chair) and placed her on her knees
before the altar. I put on a surplice[26] and stole, opened the door of the
sacrarium, closed the church, and with an appropriate number of lights
I said the entire incantation while observing her movements. I did not
see any movement to indicate obsession or possession by the Devil.
Nevertheless, in order to guard against some diabolical obsession, I
took the opportunity to remove the little ciborium[27] with the sacred
viaticum[28] from the sacrarium and placed it over her head, silently
commanding the obsessional spirits. Then I told her emphatically,
"Look, I command you in the name of Our Lord the transubstantiated
Jesus Christ and his Most Holy Mother to do no harm to that infant.
On the contrary, you are to give birth to it with good sense before
your bed because I must baptize it." Having prayed a gospel and
two prayers to the Most Holy Virgin, I finished the ceremony. The
effect must have made her aware of the protection of the Great Queen
because a few days later she gave birth to a girl with much good

sense as I commanded her to do. I baptized the child in the parish of Veracruz and the mother did not again manifest the absurdities my compadre described. All of this was at the beginning of August 1744.

No. 43. The year 1744, miracle with the print. On September 17, the day of the sacred wounds of Our Seraphic Father, I was passing by the guard post at the city gate. There I spoke to Don Francisco Xavier Lozano, brother of the esteemed Dr. Lozano, pastor of the Veracruz parish, who sadly told me that his sixteen-year-old son was dying from a virulent attack of typhus. Since he had to stand watch at the city gate, he could do no more than await the final news, for his son was in the midst of a severe attack, his eyes lifeless and his attentive physician expressing no hope. I gave him a print of the Holy Mother, asking him how he could have forgotten to offer himself to her, knowing the reputation for marvels worked by her intercession. I told him to leave his post in the hands of his companion for a while, go to the dying youth, and put the print on him with sincere faith and resignation, making Our Lady some promise in her honor and hope that with her intercession the youth would not die from the illness. He went, and as soon as he put the print in place the dying youth began to recover until he became well. The said father of the youth and his companion, Don Manuel Sousa, who was the other guard, promised me that they would swear to this miracle. I swear to what is written here in verbo sacerdotis. The father showed me his convalescing son and told me that this was the youth who owed his health to Our Lady, and that as soon as he was strong enough he would go to her temple to give her thanks [p. 34].

No. 44. The year 1744, with the print. On October 4, Juana de Dios, the two-year-old daughter of this same guard Don Francisco Xavier Lozano, suffered a mortal attack of wryneck. Already lifeless at eleven in the evening, senseless and without movement, her father entrusted her to Our Lady of Intercession. Offering the child to her from the depths of his heart, he placed the print on her and immediately the child sat up safe and sound. This event startled those present even more than the recovery of the other child described above.

No. 45. The year 1744, miracle with the print. María de los Dolores, wife of Joseph Osorio, a Mexico City Indian, went to Nativitas one day with her husband. That night the mare she had borrowed for the trip ran away. The Indians told her of the miracles that Our Lady was working and the said María de los Dolores put a candle near her print the very hour she missed the animal which, going to its favorite spot in Mexico City, was caught on the road by some muleteers who were on their way to San Angel. Félix de Santa María, in whose house the said María and her husband were staying, went to the city gate at about daybreak to see if the mare had been found. An Indian told the said Félix that he had seen some muleteers taking the mare on the road to San Angel. At this point the unfolding events testified to a miracle because the mare separated itself from the muleteers' mules and they could not recapture it. The mare again ran to its favorite spot in Mexico City precisely to present itself to the Indian Félix who tied it up at the city gate and brought it to his guests, who gave thanks for the discovery to Our Lady who did not leave unanswered the fervent faith with which the said María de los Dolores lit the candle in front of her print. The said Félix told me this and brought the said woman to me.

No. 46. To this point thirty-two miracles of Our Lady through her Most Holy Image of the Intercession are arranged by years, months, and days. Fourteen of them, worked by the Sovereign Queen in 1744, begin at page 26, no. 32; eighteen go from page 11 and no. 12 to page 20 no. 24, counting the first miracle (page 6, no. 7) in which she saved the little son of the man who restored her holy image in 1739; the other seventeen date from 1743. In addition to these cases, which I witnessed (as I make evident in the descriptions), it is clear on page 9 in the entire entry no. 10 that the mere survival of the convent in 1743 was a miracle of Divine Providence. About the events described on page 10, no. 11, and my recovery after I arrived in poor health, good judgment will say they were miraculous acts of the Most Holy Mary's intercession so that such an unworthy instrument as I consider myself to be could promote what I describe in no. 12. What is recounted in no. 17 (the escape from harm of the masons and other workers involved when the walls collapsed) is a manifest marvel. Finally, those who read [p. 35] and meditate on the events that occurred in the rebuilding of that poor convent and the means God devised for the restoration and greater devotion to Most Holy Mary through her holy image (as described on pages 4–5 nos. 4–6) will regard them as miracles of the Sovereign Queen who wished her advocation of the Intercession to be known in that pueblo and in this city. This advocation was not known anywhere until 1739, 1740, 1743, and 1744 when she revealed her pious advocation with stupendous marvels not only through her most beautiful and adorable image, but also by means of her prints. I swear to all of these in verbo sacerdotis as a witness to them, ready at any time to bear witness (if they were in need of authentication) before the Vicar General of this archdiocese. For the honor and glory of the Most Holy Virgin and deference and veneration of her Holy Image of the Intercession, I attest and offer as true testimony of all that is contained here, word for word, in the

accounts that are noted and cited in the present paragraph no. 46. I sign
it in this convent of Our Holy Father St. Francis on November 21, 1775.

Here I make my mark in witness to the truth.

Fray Francisco Antonio de la Rosa Figueroa Apostolic
Notary and Notary of the Holy Office.

Here it is appropriate to refer in a summary way to the progress in
the construction project up to July 1745, and the costs and expenses
incurred relative to it and to enhancing the dignity of the Divine Cult,
in addition to those that are registered in the inventory I cited at the
beginning on page 3 no. 3.

In the middle of October 1744 I no longer had the aid and favor of
Our Very Reverend Father Navarrete; I was subjected to the will of the
pueblo because in that month the office of commissary passed to Our
Very Reverend Father Fray Juan Fogueras. The special shade provided
by Vicar General Don Joseph Ramírez was no longer there for me
because his delicate conscience led him to resign the position. Dr. Don
Juan Joseph de la Mota succeeded him, but I never had any contact
with the new vicar general. Under this new regime I sought to bring
this most miraculous image of Our Lady to Mexico City again, but to
do so a license from the new vicar general was needed. As soon as the
Indians learned of my intentions they opposed me on the pretext that
the Most Holy Image belonged to the pueblo, that this was why they
contributed to its restoration. They made this charge before the vicar
general, alleging that when Dr. Ramírez had blessed the image he had
ordered that it not be removed from its niche thereafter. I was unable
to obtain the necessary license from Dr. Mota; since he was new to the
office he became a partisan of the Indians. Considering that I had a
large inventory of stone, tezontle, brick, rubble, lumber, ropes, and
[p. 36] hardware, and that the rebuilding would have to be suspended
for lack of lime and money to pay skilled laborers and my expenses
in the convent for carpenters, quarrymen, and tailors, I sought to go
into debt for about 350 pesos so that the work could continue until
July. This was two months before the meeting of the provincial chapter
in which I hoped that the evaluation of my work would warrant my
continuation. Finding myself in debt, under which circumstances
Our Very Reverend Father Navarrete had provided that the Syndic

should sell the precious jewels that had been collected for Our Lady at my request so that the work would not stop, I decided to sell them in order to remove the debt and not leave the chapter encumbered by the convent. As soon as the Indians learned of this plan they, quarrelsome and conceited, went before the Vicar General, who ordered me to present the jewels given to Our Lady. Along with the jewels, I presented him with such a convincing written account that he had no reason to contradict me, and in my presence he told the Indians that he would not become involved with what should be done with these jewels because it was a matter for my Franciscan prelate to decide. Under these circumstances the chapter meeting was held on September 4, 1745, and Fray Bernardo Arratia was elected Provincial. He had been an eyewitness to my honest zeal for the year and a half that he was assistant pastor at the convent of San Andrés Tetecpilco. Now distancing himself from our friendship and the fact that we had been classmates, he rendered me justice. Seeing that my hopes of finishing the construction were in limbo, this Reverend Father viewed the events with the greatest sympathy. Not only did he gather in all the jewels that I acquired, but he had them evaluated and sold by the Syndic General so that my debt of over 330 pesos owed to various people would be covered. In order to better confirm my honorable dealings, he decided that when the bills I presented were paid by the Syndic to my creditors, receipts should be made out and given to me so that what this Reverend Father decided on my behalf would be documented for all time. Our Very Reverend Father Fogueras having appointed me Reader of Nahuatl in this monastery, the guardian, Our Father Fray Pablo Antonio Pérez, welcomed me into his shade and Our Father Arratia assigned me six pesos a month for the maintenance of my father, who died the following year.

Here my gratitude requires me to affirm how much these prelates and the entire community honored both my deceased father and me. I was in the greatest poverty with no funds to pay for the funeral, not even half a real, so I went to the Reverend Father solicitor general who lent me forty pesos. I took twenty of them to Our Father the guardian [p. 37] for my father's funeral, but he gave me a good snort and would not take them. He arranged the funeral with the whole community present. The Father Sacristan Fray Christóval de Baena would not take the twelve pesos. He returned them to me, and Dr. Ramírez who was the pastor of the cathedral that week had a casket fit for four bodies brought. He outdid himself in kindness because when I went to him gently lamenting my grief and poverty he refused the thirty pesos I gave him and would only accept twelve. And his love did not stop there.

At four in the afternoon he entered the chapel of the Third Order and led me to the place of honor on the mourners' bench, saying out loud, "Now you will see the kind of funeral we prepared for your father." Shortly thereafter, fifty priests entered and part of the cathedral choir who this gentleman invited intoned the response. He accompanied me and presided over the mourning. A sergeant and intimate friend of mine who I invited to the funeral accompanied me and brought with him a good number of soldiers in order to honor my deceased father who, having twice been an alcalde mayor, was a military commander.

The jewels of gold, pearls, and precious stones sold by the Syndic General and appraised by Master Don Francisco Bruno de la Mora:

A magnificent and very distinctive string of pearls weighing one and an eighth ounces, with crested pearls, gold beads, and a little pendant a splendid emerald	100 pesos
A pair of gold earrings like little baskets, very distinctive	20 pesos
A fine gold circlet ring with emeralds	18 pesos
A circlet ring with a stone called aventurin	4 pesos
A beautiful circlet ring with diamonds	50 pesos
A pair of magnificent gold earrings with fine emeralds	70 pesos
Some pearl and garnet bracelets	20 pesos
A gold cross and little medals; four thick tombac rings made of gold; a gold ring with five turns; a gold circlet ring set with Bohemian stones; six little gold flutes; a gold cup with three little stones; a circlet ring with one green stone and two white stones. The weight of this gold without the little stones was 16 castellanos or 32 pesos. The workmanship was valued at 16 pesos; in all worth	48 pesos
A little lacquer trunk from China, one-fourth vara long, one-sixth vara wide, with a silver latch and hinges, and an iron lock and key	6 pesos
This jewelry totaled	336 pesos

The Syndic paid my bills with the proceeds and collected the receipts, which he presented to Our Father Provincial [p. 38].

Expenses I undertook in making progress on the construction of the convent and church (if God had allowed me to do it I would have done more) as well as for the Divine Cult and support of the Father Assistant:

Without encumbering the Indians I arranged for a good oven for baking bricks to be built in the pueblo because there was much very good clay, both to supply the construction project and sell in Mexico City for reinvestment in the construction. The Indians of the pueblo were paid for their labor and for transportation when other muleteers did not go there to buy it. I built at no cost to the pueblo a new shrine facing the cemetery on the main road. It was a venerable work made of rubble rock, four varas wide, three and a half varas high, and three varas in depth, with its burnished altar made of rubble and fine mortar. Over the altar there was a canvas three and a half varas wide and two and a half varas high with an oil painting depicting the most miraculous image of Our Lady flanked by Our Father St. Francis and St. Anthony. The altar was adorned with a frontal, tablecloths, and bouquets. It had a stout beveled and railed door, and to guard against vandalism at night I arranged for a very exquisite secret combination lock with a triangular slot, and a triangular key half the length of a wine glass. And I placed inside an alms box that was well secured with a lock in order to collect from travelers what God might provide.

I arranged for the very fine engraving of the Sovereign Queen's portrait beautifully sculpted by Master Conchoso [Troncoso], which Don Francisco Unzueta sponsored, as I say on page 21 no. 25, with which 4,000 prints were made.

Another plate was worked in tin for Brother Fray Agustín Zuleta or other alms collectors, for which a tinplate was fashioned for a panel and frame to fit over the money box and hold the portrait of Our Lady painted in oil, with its glass front.

With these projects and others I had in mind for an alms-collecting priest to go to the mining camps with a sponsoring travel warrant from Our Father the Provincial, the convent would have been completed and a new temple erected, but God disposed otherwise and brought me in my obedience to this convent in Mexico City to undertake during the thirty years I have lived here many projects that the prelates have assigned to my small talents, including two terms as Lector of the Mexican Language, twenty-six years as librarian, twenty-two years as archivist of this Holy Province, and twice examiner of all the bequests and pious works possessed by the province. Since the notebook I cite at the beginning on page 3 contains a list of the collections amounting to over 3,000 pesos that were added when I first obediently served in that convent in 1739 and 1740 [p. 39], I should copy from my notes the summary account I made in that convent in 1745 of the costs of the building project and expenses relative to it from 1743 during my second appointment there. The expenses for building materials were recorded for me by the master of the project, Don Joseph Gonzales.

Regarding the number of vara and a half cedar posts for the foundations, covering a staked area of 119 square varas, and 95 varas of corners for foundations using vara-and-a-quarter-wide posts required 2,400 cut posts joined together in 600 bundles of six-vara lengths, amounting to twenty posts per square vara (although in places more were needed). Twenty-four wagon loads were required, each load holding 25 bundles, and 100 bundles costing 25 pesos. The total cost (not counting transportation costs) was	600 pesos
Covering the foundations from end to end required another 100 bundles of posts	25 pesos
Freight costs ran one peso a load (it was normally two pesos, but the owners donated the difference)	25 pesos
The walls, with foundations and everything else needed for 95 varas of foundation raised to the first floor (77 varas of flat foundation and 18 with large pilasters); 925 cubic varas of hard stone and tezontle were used (excluding rubble), including 154 varas of stone and tezontle to fill the excavation for the foundations which was three varas deep and one and a quarter varas wide; and for the arches of the entryway up to the large pilaster at the corner, one and a third varas wide, 100 yards of hard stone and 14 yards of tezontle were used. The hard stone, at four pesos a yard, for 100 yards cost	400 pesos
The fourteen yards of tezontle at six pesos a yard was	84 pesos
Although half a yard of rubble and iron wall supports are normally needed for four yards of stone and tezontle, 19 yards were required at 3 pesos each, totaling	57 pesos
For the lime used in the foundations and new walls alone, 925 cubic varas were used (thirty-seven loads at twenty cubic varas of wall per load). Although I purchased some at 20 pesos, most cost 24–25 pesos because the lime venders would not bring it without a two-peso surcharge for the extra distance, so that the 37 loads cost	800 pesos
The stonework and all cost	150 pesos

For new wood, timbers, and other cedar pieces	170 pesos
The weekly payrolls for trowel masons and laborers on the foundations and walls totaled	1,000 pesos
[p. 40] Brought forward from the previous page:	3,311 pesos
Hardware and construction equipment including bricklayers' hammers, pails, trowels, trench hoes, shovels, crates, and ropes	80 pesos
The carpenter who worked for thirteen months earning three reales a day plus dinner, supper, and chocolate	234 pesos
The foreman who worked eighteenth months and the stonemason who worked two months each earned 4 reales plus dinner, supper, etc.	260 pesos
The construction of the oven, the making of the brick, firewood to burn it, transportation of the brick to Mexico City, master, workers, and fleets of mules, even though the cost was subtracted, amounted to	340 pesos
The work crews that came from Mexico City on holidays, usually twelve or more masons, were paid an additional gratuity of about	60 pesos
The wood I gathered in donations to reinforce the convent were worth	80 pesos
Six months before undertaking the construction about 500 pesos were spent in vain on rubblework walls in the basements, blind arch supports for the entrance in the interior corner, and new ceilings for the cells and office to counteract the danger to the convent. Although the tezontle, bricks, and wood used in the construction were salvaged after the demolition, at least 300 pesos for lime and the payroll of masons, workers, and the carpenter should be included in this account	300 pesos
In addition to the main construction 100 pesos were spent on lime, stone, paint, masons, stout door, lock, the painting, and decorations to build and furnish the chapel, as I have said above on page 38	100 pesos
The total spent on the construction and related expenses to this point amounts to	4,765 pesos
Besides these expenses there were others related to the construction as well as to the Divine Cult and the convent.	

The preparation of the engraved plate and the printing of about 4,000 copies cost	90 pesos
The preparation of the tin plate, printing of copies, and the framed panel for the alms box described above on page 38 amounted to about	50 pesos
The plans for the convent and the building were made by master builder Gonzales for virtually no fee	20 pesos
The very solemn Rosary for Our Lady cost	80 pesos
The printing of the sonnet on 4,000 invitations	30 pesos
Three cart loads of lime that I had paid for	60 pesos
[p. 41] Expenses carried over from the preceding page	330 pesos
Ten yards of hard stone and two of tezontle were left over	48 pesos
Assorted nails, new keys and locks, and repair of the old latches and knockers, about	50 pesos
I left about 30 pesos worth of bills to pay on the project	30 pesos
Various improvements for the Divine Cult and altars in 1744 were	50 pesos
There were besides about 2,000 pesos recorded in the inventory kept in the archive, which I left from 1739–1740, not including the jewels I collected for the Most Holy Virgin that were worth 336 pesos (evaluated above on page 37) because the price for which the Syndic sold them was the same as I owed and consumed in the costs of construction.	
But other jewels that were not gold, but rather ritual and ornamental items belonging to the Most Holy Image were worth about	100 pesos
From this I deduce that these collections and expenses relative to the construction totaled 608 pesos in 1745.	608 pesos
Adding the sum noted above	4,765 pesos
The construction and income totaled	5,373 pesos

In addition to compiling these accounts of the cost of construction and increase in capital during my second appointment to that convent from 1743 to September 1745 (when I left for this convent in Mexico City), I decided as I was writing this in 1775 to make a clean summary of my notes about the stupendous marvels and miracles of Our Lady, including the ones by means of the print of her Most Holy Image of the Intercession, all of which I witnessed. I felt in my heart a great pity that the history of these miracles would remain hidden and cast aside in this archive of the Holy Province now that that convent has been secularized. With this in mind, I felt the force of a tremendous, secret impulse that has left me no peace for the past two months, looking for ways and means to promote the cult of that most miraculous beauty on which I spent so much zeal and effort to make known and venerated throughout this city. Considering on one side the slumber or extinction of that fervor with which Mexico City once venerated and invoked her sponsorship for her miracles, on another side the decadence of her cult among the Indians of that pueblo, and on a third side the ignorance [p. 42] of the esteemed pastor of that parish and his vicario[29] about this history through lack of notice, I devised this way (inspired by the Sovereign Queen, I believe) to make these gentlemen aware of the celestial pearl preserved in the poor shell of that church. For this purpose I have undertaken the pleasant work of copying exactly what is written here so that the valuable monuments of the past contained in this archive will not come to nothing, intending to have the copy sent to the said esteemed pastor or his vicario so that they can better promote what I had in mind to do in 1744, which was to undertake authentication proceedings before the Vicar General. Once authenticated, I was going to try to find a Maecenas[30] among my benefactors to sponsor a little book that, once published, would be used to promote devotion to the advocation of the Intercession of Most Holy Mary. I had also hoped to see her temple converted in veneration into an official sanctuary. Since I can no longer do so, my burning love for the Sovereign Queen is consoled in part as I recover my spirits by writing out my old thoughts and making known to the esteemed pastor of the parish that if he has the engraved plate that I left in 1745 (which the friar who turned over the doctrina to the archdiocese in 1770 would have left), I could find a benefactor who would have a large number of prints made. From such prints Our Lady worked prodigious miracles, as I show in paragraph numbers 29, 34, 36, 38, 39, 40, 41, 43, 44, and 45 of the present narration. So, if the said plate still exists, may the esteemed pastor or his esteemed vicario be so kind as to send it to me with someone they trust or who I would send, for safekeeping while the printing was done. By means of the prints that I will send him, the veneration and cult of that most beautiful and most miraculous image will revive, and perhaps new miracles, too (of which I have no doubt). To date as I write this on January 10, 1776, the Sovereign Queen performed the following two additional miracles by means of her engraved image, which I lent and which is the only one I have left:

Francisco Antonio Ordaz, a creole Spaniard from Pachuca married to Ana María Salamanca, lives in the alleyway next to the little Plaza de San Juan in a tenement house called del Castillito. This poor, humble man lives from the scraps of food some friars give him in the infirmary (and now he lacks even this relief). Seeing that I myself was no longer able to keep my cell in order (since he has been a witness to my illnesses), six months ago he offered to help me as best he [p. 43] could in return for a little relief for him and his poor wife from the dinner and supper I have left over—the bread and a little chocolate that I give them. On various occasions he has lamented his difficulties to me. One of them was that he had a little two-year-old son who in innocent mischief put a garbanzo bean into one of his nostrils and with a little finger shoved it into the cartilage where it stuck. It swelled and caused the child terrible headaches. His parents thought it was an inflammation inside the nose, and the good man went to the father pharmacist who gave him a little apple ointment and told him to apply it inside the nostril with a small feather. In doing this a great deal of pus came out and the little boy would not let anyone near him, defending himself with annoying shouts. He was in this state for almost three months. His mother put him in the sun to see what was inside his nose and she discovered that it was a garbanzo, but neither with caresses nor reassuring words could she persuade him to let anyone probe it. For this poor man's benefit I recounted some of the miracles of Our Lady of Intercession that I write about here. In hearing them he was aflame with devotion and declared he would go to her temple with the boy and present him to the Most Holy Image. That Tuesday, January 3, 1776, at 5:00 p.m., seeing how agitated he was, I lent him the only print I had left. I told him that he and has wife should take it for a certainty that in placing the print on the child's nose and head, he would either expel the garbanzo himself or would not resist having it removed. To this end they entrusted him and themselves to Our Lady that night, placed a candle on the print, and repeatedly put it on the boy. At nine o'clock the next day, a neighbor woman came by. With reassuring words she coaxed him into the sunlight. Then she touched him with the print and, using the head of a pin, got the garbanzo to come out right away—the garbanzo that had been as impossible to extract—as easily as it had been to lodge it in the child's nostril. That night and the following morning the father observed his son, still not old enough to speak, giving signs of love and devotion to the print, kissing it and placing it on his face. Clearly the Most Holy Virgin must have been pleased by these innocent acts of love for she cured this child so quickly, to the amazement of the neighborhood. At about eleven o'clock when Francisco came to help me he recounted with astonishment all that I have said here, bringing to me the particle his son expelled, wrapped in a piece of paper. It was so hard it seemed more like a cherry pit than [p. 44] a garbanzo. It is now in my possession waiting to bear witness when needed. I swear to all that is said here in verbo sacerdotis, and for added weight I certify and attest to it as an apostolic notary.

In addition to what I have already said, I also certify and attest that, having recounted to me the miracle of the Most Holy Virgin through her print, Francisco added that on Tuesday night between seven and eight o'clock María Josepha Gutiérrez came to his room completely terrified and frightened. She begged him to go to her room because her adult daughter, María Gutiérrez de las Nieves, had fallen to the floor as if dead. Francisco went there and lifted her from the floor. This required considerable effort because she was as rigid as a tree trunk. While he was holding her by the shoulders against his chest she suffered a furious attack like a heart attack, which she had never suffered before. She recovered consciousness, but could not speak. They put her down on her back and soon she came to, shouting furiously because she felt she was dying from the intense stomach pain that was overwhelming her. Finding no quick remedy at hand in these straits, Francisco's wife, who was also there, exhorted her to invoke the intercession of Most Holy Mary while she went to her room for the engraving. Francisco took it to her, and as soon as the afflicted woman received it, she kissed it while invoking the Sovereign Queen, and placed the engraving on her stomach. The pain subsided and she was completely well and healthy.

NOTES

Introduction

1. *Las Siete Partidas*, the thirteenth-century Castilian legal text, provided a standard definition of a miracle as it would have been understood in early modern Spain and Spanish America: "a marvel worked by God, which exceeds nature in everyday experience, and therefore happens rarely. And to be considered a true miracle, four things are needed: first, that it comes through the power of God, not by other means [*arte*]; second, that the miracle is contrary to nature, otherwise people will not marvel at it; third, that the person or persons favored by God with miracles are worthy, by their saintliness and goodness; and fourth, that the miracle is such that it confirms Christian faith" (1–4, 124).

2. *Medieval Popular Culture: Problems of Belief and Perception*, János M. Bak and Paul A. Hollingsoworth, trans. (Cambridge, UK: Cambridge University Press, 1988), p. 37.

3. Philip M. Soergel, *Wondrous in His Saints: Counter-Reformation Propaganda in Bavaria* (Berkeley: University of California Press, 1993), chapter 5. Based on information about 3,126 European shrines, Mary Lee and Sidney Nolan describe seven types of origin stories, *Christian Pilgrimage in Modern Western Europe* (Chapel Hill: University of North Carolina Press, 1989), pp. 216–90. Again, at least a few examples of nearly all of their types can be found in America, but the distribution was substantially different.

4. They include the cross of Huatulco, Our Lady of La Bala, and Our Lady of La Macana.

5. William A. Christian, Jr., *Apparitions in Late Medieval and Renaissance Spain* (Princeton: Princeton University Press, 1981), chap. 1 and pp. 208–9.

6. Kenneth L. Woodward, *The Book of Miracles: The Meaning of the Miracle Stories in Christianity, Judaism, Buddhism, Hinduism, and Islam* (New York: Simon & Schuster, 2000), p. 26.

7. Preface to *November Boughs* (Philadelphia, Pa.: D. McKay, 1888).

PART I

Trouble with Miracles

1. My thanks to Inga Clendinnen, Brian Connaughton, Leslie Peirce, Paul Ramírez, Sylvia Sellers-García, Yuri Slezkine, and Wen-hsin Yeh for their thoughts about the document discussed in this essay.

2. *Obras escogidas* (Madrid: Atlas, 1961), IV, p. 373.

3. For example, Raymond Van Dam, *Saints and Their Miracles in Late Antique Gaul* (Princeton: Princeton University Press, 1993) draws on four fifth-century "books" recounting approximately 250 miracles for St. Martin of Tours; *The Book of Sainte Foy*, translated and edited by Pamela Sheingorn (Philadelphia: University of Pennsylvania Press, 1995), records 116 miracle stories from the early eleventh century; the Castilian

text, *Cántigas de Santa María* offers 357 different miracles (available in English translation by Kathleen Kulp-Hill as *Songs of Holy Mary of Alfonso X, the Wise* [Tempe: Arizona
Center for Medieval and Renaissance Studies, 2000]).

4. In his recent book about five celebrated miracles from the Spanish Nether-
lands, *Miracles at the Jesus Oak: Histories of the Supernatural in Reformation Europe* (New
York: Doubleday, 2003), pp. 4–5.

5. Philip M. Soergel, *Wondrous in His Saints: Counter-Reformation Propaganda
in Bavaria* (Berkeley: University of California Press, 1993), p. 103; Benedicta Ward,
Miracles and the Medieval Mind: Theory, Record and Event, 1000–1215 (Philadelphia:
University of Pennsylvania Press, 1987), drew from 150 miracles worked by relics of
Thomas á Becket at Canterbury during the seven-year period, 1171–1177; Françoise
Crémoux studied 747 episodes from the miracle books of the shrine of Guadalupe
(Spain) recorded between 1510 and 1599, *Pélerinages et miracles á Guadalupe au XVIe
siècle* (Madrid: Casa de Velásquez, 2001).

6. *Canons and Decrees of the Council of Trent*, H. J. Schroeder, trans. (St. Louis, Mo.:
B. Herder Book Co., 1941).

7. Francisco de Florencia, *Zodíaco mariano . . . los templos y lugares dedicados
a los cultos de su S.S. Madre por medio de las más célebres y milagrosas imágenes de
la misma Señora, que se veneran en esta América Septentrional, y Reynos de la Nueva
España*, edited with additions by Juan Antonio de Oviedo, S.J. (Mexico: Colegio
de San Ildefonso, 1755), pp. 9, 32, 33, 41, 50, 56, 60, consulted or referenced such
informaciones jurídicas for the Marian shrines of La Conquistadora (Puebla,
1582), Zapopan (Jalisco, 1641, 1653, 1663), Cosamaloapan (Veracruz, 1641 or 1642),
Nuestra Señora del Pueblito (Querétaro, 1649), Nuestra Señora de la Laguna
(Yucatán, 1649), Nuestra Señora de Guadalupe (1666), Nuestra Señora de San
Juan de los Lagos (Jalisco, 1668, 1693), and Nuestra Señora de la Salud (Pátzcuaro,
1739). For an example of a lengthy investigation into a reported miracle and
its suppression (this one from the 1670s and 1680s), see Martha Lilia Tenorio,
De panes y sermones: El milagro de los "panecitos" de Santa Teresa (Mexico: El Colegio
de México, 2002).

8. Early published compendia for Mexico include Luis de Cisneros, *Historia
de el principio y origen progressos venidas a Mexico, y milagros de la Santa Ymagen de
nuestra Señora de los Remedios, extramuros de Mexico . . .* (Mexico: Iuan Blanco de
Alcaçar, 1621); Bernardo de Lizana, *Devocionario de Nuestra Señora de Izamal y con-
quista espiritual* (Valladolid: Gerónimo Morillo, 1633); Miguel Sánchez, *Imagen de la
virgen María Madre de Dios de Gvadalvpe, milagrosamente aparecida en la civdad de Mexico*
(Mexico: Imprenta de Bernardo Calderón, 1648); and Francisco de Florencia and
Juan Antonio Oviedo's *Zodíaco mariano . . .* (Mexico: Imprenta del Colegio de San
Ildefonso, 1755), much of it compiled by Florencia in the late seventeenth century.
For Spain, examples include Narciso Camós, O.P., *Jardín de María plantada en el prin-
cipado de Cataluña* (1657) (Barcelona: Editorial Orbis, 1949), which offers a smattering of miracle stories but mainly concerns the shrines; Roque Alberto Faci, *Aragón,
reyno de Christo, y dote de Maria SS.ma fundado sobre la columna inmobil de Nuestra
Señora en su ciudad de Zaragoza* (Zaragoza: Joseph Fort, 1739), treats 104 images, again
with a smattering of miracle stories; and Juan de Villafañe, *Compendio histórico, en
que se da noticia de las milagrosas y devotas imágenes de la reyna de cielos y tierra . . .
que se veneran en los más célebres santuarios de España* (Madrid: M. Fernández, 1740),
surveys eighty-five Spanish Marian shrines. Of the chapters I read for ten shrines, 112
miracles were recounted, for an average of eleven miracles each. By contrast, a mid-
sixteenth-century book of the history and miracles of Nuestra Señora de Montserrat
recounted 239 miracles for this one shrine alone, *Libro de la historia y milagros hechos a
invocación de Nuestra Señora de Montserrat* (Barcelona: Pedro Monpezat, 1550).

9. Émile Durkheim, *The Elementary Forms of Religious Life*, Carol Cosman, trans. (Oxford: Oxford University Press, 2001), pp. 180n1, 237, 239–40.

10. "Yet another distinguishing quality of the priest, it is asserted, is his professional equipment of special knowledge, fixed doctrine, and vocational qualifications, which brings him into contrast with sorcerers, prophets, and other types of religious functionaries who exert their influence by virtue of personal gifts (charisma) made manifest in miracle and revelation"; "the perpetual control of an individual's life pattern by the official, whether father confessor or spiritual director, empowered to distribute grace, a control that in certain respects is very effective, is in practice very often cancelled by the circumstance that there is always grace remaining to be distributed anew," Max Weber, *The Sociology of Religion*, Ephraim Fischoff, trans. (Boston, Mass.: Beacon Press, 1963), pp. 29, 189.

11. In *Zodíaco mariano*, p. 62, Florencia or Oviedo claimed that there had been a book of about three hundred miracles for the shrine of Nuestra Señora de San Juan de los Lagos, now lost. I hope to have more to say on another occasion about why there were no miracle books in colonial Mexico, and why comparatively few Mexican miracles were recorded for posterity.

12. For example, Cisneros, *Historia de el principio*, 129r-v, 135.

13. "A esta epidemia de olvido acude con el remedio de la historia," Jesuit Joseph Ramírez's *sentir* at the beginning of Francisco de Florencia's *La milagrosa invención de un tesoro escondido . . .* (Mexico: Viuda de Juan de Ribera, 1685), pages unnumbered.

14. Kenneth L. Woodward, *The Book of Miracles: The Meaning of the Miracle Stories in Christianity, Judaism, Buddhism, Hinduism, and Islam* (New York: Simon and Schuster, 2000), p. 26.

15. Some shrines and images had specialties that complicate general patterns and reflect local circumstances. Miraculous images in coastal settlements, such as the Cristo de San Román of Campeche, were noted for rescues at sea and other maritime prodigies. Others, such as the fame of Querétaro's Nuestra Señora del Pueblito for bringing a good death to the repentant, seem less related to geography or the local economy.

16. Two contrasts to European patterns in these records may or may not stand up to close scrutiny: (1) despite the post-Tridentine skepticism about reported apparitions in the European record, at least fifty-two apparitions were reported in the Mexican ecclesiastical sources, most of them from the sixteenth and seventeenth centuries; (2) for the most part the Mexican miracle stories are less fraught with political and social danger than their European counterparts. There is little in the body of Mexican stories that is quite like the ominous social circumstances of miracles associated with St. Martin of Tours in the fifth century, St. Foye in the eleventh century, Spain's Montserrat and Guadalupe in the sixteenth century, La Salette and Marpingen in the nineteenth century, or Fatima and Medjugorje in the twentieth century.

17. Joseph Manuel Ruiz y Cervantes reported that the shrine of Nuestra Señora de Xuquila in southwestern Oaxaca displayed thousands of milagritos in the early 1780s, adding about two hundred to the collection every year, *Memorias de la portentosa imagen de Nuestra Señora de Xuquila . . .* (Mexico: F. de Zúñiga y Ontiveros, 1791).

18. *Historia de la milagrosa imagen de Nuestra Señora del Pueblito, de la santa provincia de religiosos observantes de San Pedro y San Pablo de Michoacán* (n.p., n.d.) (composed after 1747, since the last dated miracle recounted is 1747, and before 1769 when the famous— but here unmentioned—Picazo miracle occurred), p. 83, October 29, 1747. During the nineteenth and twentieth centuries ex-voto paintings, made to order in shrine towns on cheap tin sheets slightly bigger than a sheet of writing paper, were a popular expression of devotion for all but the poorest devotees in Mexico.

19. See, for example, the compact disk, "México en un espejo: Los exvotos de San Juan de los Lagos, 1870–1945" (Mexico: UNAM, 2000).

20. *Zodíaco mariano*, p. 267.

21. Two examples of captions on published ex-voto paintings that have the same form and basic content are: "On August 6, 1775, Doña María Flores found herself gravely ill from a mortal attack of apoplexy, hemorrhaging blood. Without hope of remedy, she commended herself to Our Most Holy Mother and Lady of Guadalupe and found herself safe and sound by the grace of God"; and "On October 16, 1771, Don Pedro Jurado suffered a deadly seizure and delirium. His sister Doña Antonia invoked the Archangel St. Michael, promising to come and offer him a little silver body. Don Pedro recovered from the attack and both of them came to this shrine to offer their thanks to this great Prince," *Dones y promesas: 500 años de arte ofrenda (exvotos mexicanos)* (Mexico: Centro Cultural, Fundación Cultural Televisa, A.C., 1996), pp. 56–57.

22. "The Peculiarities of the English," in *The Poverty of Theory and Other Essays* (New York: Monthly Review Press, 1978), p. 275, tellingly quoted as an epigraph in Inga Clendinnen's *Dancing with Strangers: Europeans and Australians at First Contact* (Melbourne: Text Publishing, 2003).

23. Bancroft Library MSS 87/190m, "Mexican Miscellany," carton 2.

24. Doña Josepha Francisca's marriage to Don Ignacio de Larralde, a native of the Villa de Azpeitia, Guipúzcoa, is recorded in the marriage register of the Diocese of Guadalajara on January 21, 1728, *Index to the Marriage Investigations of the Diocese of Guadalajara: Pertaining to the Former Provinces of Coahuila, Nuevo León, Nuevo Santander, and Texas,* Raúl J. Guerra, Jr., Nadine M. Vásquez, and Baldomero Vela, Jr., eds. ([Brownsville, Tex.?]: R. J. Guerra, 1989–), I, 79. Her sister's marriage to Don Juan Antonio de Sobrevilla y Layseca from the province of Álava appears on p. 106 of this index. Members of the prominent Garza family appear among witnesses in the records for the Cantú del Río y la Zerda family.

25. In their attention to Doña María Francisca's mental and emotional state, the bishop and his learned advisers may well have taken a cue from the widely distributed and influential text, *De Servorum Dei beatificatione et Beatorum canonizatione*, by Prospero Lambertini (who would go on to become Pope Benedict XIV, 1740–1758), which was published in five volumes between 1734 and 1738. In Lambertini's view, visions and apparitions had three possible origins: natural, diabolical, and divine, of which only the last was a genuine sign from God. "Natural" visions were the result of illness or mental instability, especially "if the ecstasy be succeeded by weariness, sluggishness of the limbs, a clouding of the mind and understanding, forgetfulness of past events, paleness of face and sadness of mind" (described and quoted by Kenneth L. Woodward in *Making Saints* [New York: Simon & Schuster, 1990], p. 169).

26. *Ecstatic Religion: A Study of Shamanism and Spirit Possession*, 2nd ed. (London: Routledge, 1989), pp. 26–27.

27. The name change seems less mysterious. Oak trees had a special appeal as sites of miracles, as William Christian has noticed for Spain since early modern times: "Apple trees and blackberry bushes quickly were abandoned (as 'the' vision site) for oak trees," "Six Hundred Years of Visionaries in Spain: Those Believed and Those Ignored," in Michael P. Hanagan, Leslie Page Moch, and Wayne Te Brake, eds., *Challenging Authority: The Historical Study of Contentious Politics* (Minneapolis: University of Minnesota Press, 1998), p. 117. "Our Lady of the Oak Tree" appears often as a special advocation of Mary in Camós and other Marian compendia for early modern Spain, but they rarely mention other trees. And Matías de Escobar, early eighteenth-century *cronista* for the Augustinian Province of San Nicolás Tolentino de Mechoacán in western Mexico, had something to say about the oak's special appeal. "The oak tree," he wrote, "is an evergreen that gives us shade and nourishment, and is our defense," *Americana Thebaida* (1729) (Morelia: Balsal Editores, 1970), p. 464.

28. Hartmut Lehmann's lecture at the University of California, Berkeley, in April 2004 explored this theme of miracles in catastrophes in early modern Germany. Benito Jerónimo Feijóo's skepticism within belief suggests a more rigorous standard for judging miracles in eighteenth-century Spain, but one that stopped short of the disenchantment Lehmann notices: "[Here] is the way I proceed in this matter: to believe those miracles which are well authenticated, to doubt those which do not possess strong evidence, and to judge those false which after careful examination I have judged to be such. . . . Am I convinced by the number of witnesses? No, by the quality." Quoted in Lee Hoinacki, *El Camino: Walking to Santiago de Compostela* (University Park: Pennsylvania State University Press, 1996), p. 228.

29. I have not searched the burial registers of Monterrey for the date of her death.

30. For example, Francisco de Florencia in *La milagrosa invención* asserted that although there was little documentation on the early history of the shrine of Our Lady of los Remedios and the many miraculous cures there, any doubts were erased by the fact that they were widely retold and known in the voz pública y fama. "Los milagros de esta Imagen son vozes que la publican" (The miracles of this image are themselves voices that publicize it), he wrote in chapter 1, and reiterated in chapter 2: "tenemos por ciertas solo con fe humana" (human faith alone makes them certain).

31. William Christian makes the point of the fittingness and familiarity of a miracle story being important to its acceptance by the laity and church authorities, in "Six Hundred Years of Visionaries in Spain," pp. 116–17.

32. *The History Primer* (New York: Basic Books, 1971), p. 169.

Document: Summary investigation concerning the marvel that Our Lady of the Walnut Tree worked for Doña María Francisca Larralde

1. The feast of Our Lady of Expectation on December 18 commemorates a mini-annunciation seven days before the birth of Christ in which an angel greets the pregnant Mary: "Rejoice, the Lord is with you" (Luke 1:29). In this advocation, Mary is depicted deep in contemplation of her son, with her hands above and below the unborn baby.

2. Licentiate—an advanced academic degree beyond *bachiller* and short of *maestro* (master) and *doctor* (doctor).

3. "el que hizo *in verbo sacerdotis tacto pectore*."

4. The Nazarene—Jesus bearing the cross on the road to Calvary.

5. Communion given to a dying person.

6. Her brother sometimes is referred to in these records as the vicario juez eclesiástico, but vicario may also refer to Buenaventura de la Garza who, as the lieutenant parish priest would also have been called vicario.

7. The bull is not specified.

8. It is not clear whether both spouses were to wear the Franciscan habit. In the context of Doña María Francisca's earlier request of her husband that he wear it next to his skin, the order here would seem to apply to him.

PART II

Document: Account of the prodigious miracle by Most Holy Mary in the village of Santa María de la Asumpción Tlamacazapa

1. Is Father Mesa here reminded of the image of Notre-Dame de Grace, a medieval image in Cambrai, France, reputedly sculpted by Saint Luke?

PART III

Between Nativitas and Mexico City

1. In an earlier article I emphasized this sculpted image of the Virgin Mary and the "biography" and charismatic properties of the printed likeness de la Rosa commissioned, "Nuestra Señora del Patrocinio y Fray Francisco de la Rosa: Una intersección de religión, política, y arte en el México del siglo XVIII," *Relaciones* 73 (winter 1998): 281–312. De la Rosa's personal network of patronage, affiliation, friendship, and rivalry in Mexico City; his historical perspectives; and his labors after 1745 in the context of Franciscan history and Bourbon politics deserve more attention, too, as do his other extant writings, all of them unpublished.

2. His checkered history as a novice is documented in the library of the Instituto Nacional de Antropología e Historia (Mexico City), Fondo Franciscano, libro de informaciones de los novicios del Convento Recoleto de San Cosmé, 1704–1728, vol. 7, fols. 597–612.

3. The gist of de la Rosa's formal complaint to the Audiencia about his Indian parishioners there on May 22, 1734, would be repeated often during his eleven years of pastoral service. He expressed his frustration over their superstitions, heavy drinking, adultery, indifference to the faith, disobedience, and other signs of what he took to be the devil's work. Biblioteca Nacional, Archivo Franciscano (hereafter BN AF) caja 109 doc. 1505.

4. These assignments were in Calimaya (Valley of Toluca) in 1737 and Mazatepec (Morelos) in 1738. At Mazatepec he was at the center of a new controversy over idolatrous practices, denouncing the pueblo of Coatlan for "calling on witches to divine stolen items by ingesting peyote, pipitzintles, and other herbs," which he judged to be pacts with the devil. He directed some of his criticism toward the alcalde mayor, intimating that his failure to monitor these superstitions was motivated by personal greed, Archivo General de la Nación (hereafter AGN) Inquisición vol. 820, exp. 5, fol. 135. An appointment in modern Morelos during the eighteenth century could be a rude introduction to the ministry. See Taylor, *Magistrates of the Sacred*, appendix 3.

5. His service in Xochitepec and Santa María la Redonda from July 1740 to January 1743 was especially unhappy. He clashed with Indians and *mestizos* of Xochitepec over alleged witchcraft and denounced "the ignorance and idiocy of these people." He seems to have suffered emotionally from these conflicts. "I say that the wailings of my conscience are so profound and unceasing because the Catholic zeal of the Christian religion in the house of the Lord, which is the Holy Church, eats my heart out. I cannot rest until I put these great and stupendous abominations against Our Most Holy Faith before the exalted comprehension of this Saintly Apostolic Tribunal," he wrote to the Inquisition from Xochitepec on May 23, 1741, AGN Inquisición 820 exp. 5, fols. 134–37.

Within weeks he was reassigned to Santa María la Redonda, and bad turned to worse. By the spring of 1742 he had launched a series of judicial actions in which he complained of his new communicants' insolence, disobedience, lawlessness, and sacrilegious ways. He was ill and afraid, as well as angry over their failure to fulfill their spiritual duties or support the work of the parish. He suspected that several parishioners he had punished were plotting to kill him, and added that the district governor paid no heed, BN AF caja 141 doc. 1732, and Bancroft Library, University of California, Berkeley, M-M 135 exps. 14, 19. De la Rosa's troubles in Santa María la Redonda were not just of his own making. His predecessor there in the 1690s also reported "graves desórdenes" and other provocations, Bancroft Library M-M 135 exp. 15, 1696.

6. And he was back in court with the people of Nativitas, bringing a suit against them to the archbishop's vicar general on October 16, 1744, in response to an earlier complaint they had made against him. An apparently amicable agreement was reached

on May 24, 1745, four months before he was removed from Nativitas, Bancroft Library M-M 135 exp. 28.

7. Quick to identify shrines and miraculous images when he found them, José Antonio de Villaseñor y Sánchez did not mention this image in his paragraph about the pueblo of Nuestra Señora de Nativitas, *Suplemento al Teatro Americano: La ciudad de México en 1755* (Sevilla: Escuela de Estudios Hispanoamericanos and Mexico: UNAM, 1980), p. 116.

8. The Council of Trent decreed in its twenty-fifth session, Dec. 3–4, 1563, that "no new miracles be accepted or new relics recognized without the bishop's examination and approval." There is no sign that de la Rosa sought episcopal certification of the events he calls miracles in his text. More circumspect colonial reporters of uncertified supernatural events wrote of "marvels" and "prodigious events" (*maravillas* and *prodigios*) rather than miracles.

9. Were these miracles, or acts of magnanimity and self-interest? It was all the same to Father de la Rosa, who was inclined to find the hand of God behind everything positive that related to the promotion of Nuestra Señora del Patrocinio. The donor who served as "godfather" of the ceremonial blessing of the restored statue when it was returned to Nativitas was a gunpowder supplier who presumably saw a business opportunity as well as a chance to demonstrate his devotion to the Virgin. (BN AF caja 109, doc. 1494, para. 6. De la Rosa numbered the paragraphs of his text, not the pages.)

De la Rosa neglects to say how often his frequent appeals for supplies failed to bear fruit. One of his failures is recorded in the minutes of Mexico City's municipal council on July 7, 1743. In that session of the council his petition for "some lumber, even if it is old, a little lime, and the large quantity of stone left along the Calzada de San Antón, which the Indians can collect" was read. All but one of the eight councilors in attendance that day rejected the petition. The councilor who did not vote against the petition abstained because he served as the principal lay adviser to Franciscan convents in the city, Archivo Histórico del Distrito Federal (hereafter AHDF), número de inventario vol. 68A, fol. 75v.

10. De la Rosa's text can be read as the belated *información jurídica* that had not been compiled in the 1740s. He wrote in the text, "The authentication never took place because I was removed from the convent." It is more in the form of an *información jurídica* than a standard devotional history. The difference is illustrated by the two texts for the Cristo Renovado de Santa Teresa published in the late seventeenth century, *Renovación por sí misma* . . . (Mexico: Viuda de Francisco Rodríguez Lupercio, 1688) (an *información jurídica*) and *Exaltación de la divina misericordia en la milagrosa renovación de la soberana imagen de Christo Señor Nuestro Crucificado* . . . (Mexico: Viuda de Ribera, 1699) (first edition of the devotional history).

11. Or perhaps most were thrown away as worthless scrap paper? I suppose the print and paper are too fine, and the artist too famous, to be treated as trash.

12. His Creole spirit is especially evident in a long treatise against Archbishop Lorenzana's native languages policy, Bancroft Library M-M 101 "Vindicias de la verdad" ("Vindications of truth").

13. The twenty-one beneficiaries of the Virgin's miracles in the capital included three Creole *doñas* (women of high status), the mother of a master architect, the daughter of a *don*, a bishop's page, the son of a Spanish military man, a nun, a pharmacist, two Creole builders, a *castizo* carder, two Indians, a *mulato* laborer, a *mulata* maid, the wife of a coachman, a non-Indian woman living in a tenement, two Creoles of modest means, and a guard's daughter.

14. BN AF caja 109 doc. 1494, para. 32.

15. First in para. 3 ("You will be astonished to find in the folio inventory book that I fashioned, in file 58 of this archive, that my collections for the sacred paraphernalia

and repairs to the monastery exceeded 3,000 pesos"); then in para. 8 ("the funds total-ing more than 3,000 pesos free and clear added by me to the poor little monastery of Nativitas") and his list of collections and expenses at the end of the text.

16. This certainly was de la Rosa's opinion in 1775. Was it just a retrospective view, colored by his departure from Nativitas under duress in 1745 after his parish-ioners lodged complaints against him? I don't think so. Judging by his letters to the Inquisition and the Audiencia of Mexico in the 1730s and 1740s—before and during his tenure at Nativitas—his opinion of Indians in general and the people of Nativitas in particular were no different in 1740 than they were in 1775. Furthermore, the explana-tion in the text of why he was removed did not center on his troubles with the people of Nativitas.

17. Paras. 4, 7.

18. Bernardino de Sahagún, the great Franciscan student of Nahuatl and native tra-ditions in the mid-sixteenth century, would not have made de la Rosa's roster of heroes. According to Luis Nicolau D'Olwer, de la Rosa denounced at least one of Sahagún's Nahuatl texts (the *Psalmodia*) to the Inquisition "with such success that only 3–4 copies survive," *Bernardino de Sahagún (1499–1590)* (Salt Lake City: University of Utah Press, 1987), p. 75.

19. Not to mention paintings of the Christ of Chalma and Our Lady of La Piedad, among others.

20. In the 1690s, Vetancurt (p. 87) described Nativitas as a small *pueblo* dedicated to the Nativity of the Virgin, with three subordinate villages and an adult population of about 230 Indians and eight Spaniards. Its convent housed three Franciscans, who ministered to the spiritual needs of the Indians under the jurisdiction of the provin-cial headquarters in Mexico City.

21. BN AF caja 109, doc. 1494.

22. BN Fondo Reservado Ms 123 (1025), libro de inventarios, autos de visita, 1739–1753. A 1726 record of endowed masses at the church of Nativitas attests to enthusiastic devotion there to the Nativity and Assumption of the Virgin Mary before de la Rosa arrived, BN AF caja 92 exp. 1397.

23. Paras. 4, 5, 22.

24. This initiative is recorded in the Nativitas alms collector's petition for an official copy of his license after he was robbed of his papers and money, AGN Clero Regular y Secular 181 exp. 6, April 1808. At the time de la Rosa first went to Nativitas the church reportedly had the benefit of two small bequests producing sixty reales for an annual mass and procession. One of the benefactors was Joan Sebastián, *indio*, BN AF caja 120, doc. 1588.

25. While de la Rosa insisted on calling the statue a representation of Nuestra Señora del Patrocinio (Our Lady of Intercession), he knew that the church and image were known locally as Nuestra Señora de Nativitas. The bilingual text of Christian doc-trine he began to write at Nativitas in December 1744 identifies the place as "Convento y santuario de Nuestra Señora del Patrocinio nombrado Nativitas en el pueblo de Tepetlaltzingo extramuros de dha ciudad" ("Convent and shrine of Our Lady of Inter-cession, named Nativitas, in the pueblo of Tepetlatzingo on the outskirts of said city"), Bancroft Library M-M 100.

26. Vetancurt, p. 87, identified brickmaking; Villaseñor y Sánchez, *Suplemento*, p. 116, mentioned that people of Nativitas sold hay, salt, and saltpeter in the city. He briefly described the filtration and evaporation processes used to make the salt cakes there. Nativitas's property dispute with a rival salt miner and processor is recorded in AGN Tierras 1415 exp. 4 (1815).

27. Para. 6.

28. AHDF acta de cabildo for Dec. 7, 1739, and AGN Alcaldes Mayores 10, fols. 11–12 (1740). The willingness and ability of communities within the district of Nativitas

to litigate political disputes should also have given de la Rosa pause in his estimation of Indian ignorance and lethargy. For example, in 1709 the subject villages of San Simón Ticomán and San Andrés Tetepilco complained to the archbishop of "grave extortions and interference" from the people of Nativitas and sought to separate from the *doctrina* and have their own resident priest, BN AF caja 109 doc. 1494.

29. Throughout his career de la Rosa was quick to report to the Inquisition on suspicious practices and literature that smacked of the devil's work. For example, AGN Inquisición vol. 820 exp. 5 (1741), vol. 899 fols. 254–56 (1747), and vol. 1520 exp. 10 (1767). That the Inquisition no longer had jurisdiction over Indian affairs must have disappointed him.

30. In the Nativitas narrative Father de la Rosa was quick to criticize the record-keeping practices of others, and touchy about criticism of his own records.

31. An example is his well-researched brief of 1772 in defense of his province's right of *patronato* over the main chapel of its Mexico City monastery (*patronato* basically meant the authority to administer chapel affairs and appoint its chaplains), BN AF caja 54, doc. 1137. In 1765 he was appointed to a team of inspectors of the property and archives of the twenty *conventos* that remained to his province, BN AF caja 109 exp. 1499.

32. These changes are discussed in Taylor, *Magistrates of the Sacred*, especially chapter 1.

33. In the early 1770s he wrote at length about the threat to Christianity in New Spain posed by the new language policy, and closely followed the work of the regalist Fourth Provincial Synod in 1771. See Bancroft Library M-M 101 and M-M 69–70.

34. In another manuscript written after Easter in 1745 (near the end of his service in Nativitas), Father de la Rosa noted that for the first time many of his parishioners living in Mexico City had returned to confess and take communion in Nativitas, Bancroft Library M-M 135, exp. 28. This added interest by nonresidents in the life of the parish may be another sign of a desire to keep the statue there.

35. Benson Library, University of Texas, Manuscript No. 1641 (G-25).

36. In addition to the account of Nuestra Señora del Patrocinio, two versions of the catalogue of deceased members of the province, and various other indexes and catalogues for the menología project now in the Benson Library, his writings included a 608-page text of Christian doctrine in Spanish and Nahuatl begun during his second appointment at Nativitas, which he hoped to publish (Bancroft Library, M-M 100); a scathing treatise from the early 1770s on the regalist program to eliminate native languages from Christian practice in Mexico (Bancroft Library, M-M 101); a Nahuatl grammar; five volumes of sermons; a volume of poetry in Latin and Spanish; and various indexes and lists of proscribed books and the holdings of the library of his monastery. The grammar, sermons, poetry, and indexes are mentioned in José Mariano Beristáin de Souza, *Biblioteca hispanoamericana septentrional, o catálogo y noticias de los literatos que o nacidos o educados, o florecientes en la América septentrional española, han dado a luz algún escrito, o lo han dejado preparado para la prensa, 1521–1850*, 3rd ed. (Mexico: Ediciones Fuente Cultural, 1947), II, p. 258. Beristáin located these manuscripts in the archive of de la Rosa's monastery in Mexico City. Elisa Sampson Vera Tudela adds a two-volume manuscript "Crónica sucinta del convento de Santa Clara de México" dated 1755 that she located in the INAH library of the Museum of Anthropology in Mexico City, *Colonial Angels: Narratives of Gender and Spirituality in Mexico, 1580–1750* (Austin: University of Texas Press, 2000), p. 189.

37. In addition to the rebuilding project that began in 1807 there was at least one more major restoration, completed in 1944. The latter project is commemorated with a marble plaque on the right-hand wall just inside the doorway. The cloister area, so prominent in de la Rosa's plans, has been rebuilt and converted into a school; and a taller annex has been added behind the church.

38. I am indebted to María Isabel Estrada Torres for sharing her account of the annual fiesta and conversations with parishioners.

Document: History of Miracles Worked by the Image of Our Lady of Intercession

1. In honor of the feast day in November to celebrate her divine mediation.

2. "A house or convent of regular clergy devoted to study," *Diccionario de la lengua castellana,* 6th ed., Madrid: 1822 (hereafter *DLC*).

3. The *convento grande* of the Franciscans in Mexico City.

4. The beneficed minister or pastor of a curacy.

5. The sacrarium usually means the shallow basin placed near the altar and used for washing the communion utensils, but here and elsewhere in the document de la Rosa seems to be referring to the tabernacle housing the consecrated Host.

6. Canopy or protective covering.

7. Unit of measure, said to be three feet; usually about thirty-three inches.

8. The pueblo officials of Nativitas.

9. Business administrator of the province.

10. Giving the word of a priest.

11. Popular fermented beverage made from maguey juice.

12. *Macahuitl* or *macana*: a warrior's club studded with obsidian points. Here probably a thick club.

13. A league is about 2.6 miles or 4.2 kilometers.

14. Bermeo, a municipality in Vizcaya, Spain, had recently celebrated the five-hundredth anniversary of its founding. Perhaps some of Father de la Rosa Figueroa's benefactors were Basques. Perhaps he, too, was of Basque ancestry.

15. The portico and anteroom leading into the cloister.

16. Tezontle is a soft, red volcanic rock used extensively in construction in Mexico City during the seventeenth and eighteenth centuries.

17. Small round stones; rubble.

18. Soda ash.

19. Close friends sealed by the bond of godparenthood. The term carried the added meaning of protector and benefactor.

20. The Spanish word here is *achones,* from *hachón,* "a brazier on a tall stand lighted on special occasions of public rejoicing," *DLC* 1822.

21. *DLC*, 1822 defines mal de madre as "an ailment that causes vapors which, rising to the head, affect the nervous system and cause various serious attacks" ("afecto vaporoso que elevándose a la cabeza toca en el sistema nervioso, y causa varios accidentes de mucho cuidado").

22. A real is one-eighth of a silver peso.

23. A light-complected mestizo; theoretically, a person who was three-quarters Spanish and one-quarter Indian.

24. American-born Spaniard.

25. De la Rosa probably is referring to the *Flagellum daemonium, exorcismos terribiles* . . . , a standard handbook for exorcists by Girolamo Menghi. The first of many editions apparently was published in Bologna in 1577.

26. A half-length, long-sleeved tunic worn by all clergy.

27. A covered container used to store the consecrated wafers.

28. The Eucharist given to a dying person.

29. Assistant to the pastor (cura) of a parish or *doctrina* (proto-parish administered by one of the Mendicant orders).

30. Roman statesman, patron of Virgil and Horace.

Index

Acamixtla, 54, 57, 61, 63, 65
alcalde mayor, 72, 90, 129, 143n4
alms, 27, 74, 78, 83, 84, 94, 106–7, 109, 111, 130, 133
apparitions, visions, 2–3, 11, 53–55, 58, 59, 61–64, 139n16, 141n25
Arratia, Fr. Bernardo (Franciscan provincial), 89, 120, 128
Ave Maria, 112

baldachin, 93, 147
Basque, 15, 147n14
bells, 16, 28, 66, 94
Bermeo's jubilee, 103, 147
bishop's court, eighteenth-century activities, 1, 2, 5, 9, 10, 14, 17, 19, 20, 21, 23–24, 36, 47–49, 61, 63, 83–85, 89, 140n25, 144n12
Blessed Sacrament, 4, 16, 26, 27, 28, 30, 33–35, 37, 38, 40, 41, 43, 45, 48, 95, 106
blessing, 43, 45, 59, 95, 104, 111, 123, 124, 127, 144, 144n9
Bourbon reforms, 1, 19, 84, 86, 142n1, 146n33

Cajetan, Saint, 109
candles, liturgical uses and as offerings, 12, 59, 64, 81, 95, 103, 112, 116, 119, 125, 126, 135
castizo, 119, 144n13
Chalcatzingo, 72
chocolate, drink, 27, 29, 31, 32, 42, 132, 135
Christian, William, 4, 31, 141n27
Christianity, 1, 9, 10, 34
communion, 15, 17, 18, 29, 32, 47, 65, 80, 93, 101, 108, 122
compadre, 57, 59, 109, 119, 125
Conde de Fuenclara (viceroy), 96
confession, 27, 34, 65, 67, 73, 80, 93, 122, 126n34, 146n34
corn (maize), 53–67
Creole Spaniards, 72, 77, 121, 134, 144nn12–13

devil, demons, 2, 3, 82, 105, 107, 123, 124, 143nn3–4, 146n29
devotional histories, 10–13, 20, 75, 76, 144n10
devotional practices, 71; gestures of faith, 11, 12, 14, 35, 36, 38, 48; offerings, 12, 13, 42, 81, 83, 95, 108, 110–26 passim; prayer, 13, 18, 26, 57, 59, 81, 95, 108, 110–26 passim; veneration of saints and images, 33–35, 37, 40, 44, 54, 59, 65–66, 73, 82, 110–26 passim; vigils, 15, 18, 26, 45, 119; vows, 15–19, 23, 24, 26, 29–30, 42, 106, 108, 110–26 passim; wear Franciscan habit, 40–43. *See also* alms; blessing; communion; confession; devotional histories; ex-voto paintings; home altar; litany of Our Lady; rosary procession and altar
Díaz del Castillo, Bernal: compared to Francisco Antonio de la Rosa Figueroa, 75
doctrina (proto-parish administered by mendicant pastors), 71, 74, 82, 84, 134, 148n29
Durkheim, Émile, 10

Easter duty, 55, 65, 67
epidemic, 74, 79, 85, 92, 101
ex-voto paintings, 2, 12–14, 16, 108, 140n18, 140n21. See also *milagritos*

fast, 58, 61, 65
fire, 78, 117, 118
Flagellum Demonis, 124, 148n25
Florencia, Francisco de, 1, 138nn7–8, 139n11, 141n30
Fogueras, Fr. Juan (comisario), 127, 128
Franciscans, 5; College of San Fernando and Fernandine friars, 73, 74, 85, 90; convent in Monterrey, 15, 20, 29, 38–39, 44; embattled in the eighteenth century, 84–87; lay followers, 16–18, 20, 27, 29–30, 142n8; Province of the